SNOW, FIRE AND GOLD

The story of Bill Spargo and Evelyn Piper's life in the Australian mountains

STEPHEN WHITESIDE

First published by Busybird Publishing 2024

Copyright © 2024 Stephen Whiteside

ISBN:

Paperback: 978-1-923216-14-3

Ebook: 978-1-923216-15-0

This work is copyright. Apart from any use permitted under the *Copyright Act 1968*, no part of this publication may be reproduced, stored in a retrieval system or transmitted in any form or by any means, electronic, mechanical, photocopying, recording or otherwise, without the prior written permission of Stephen Whiteside.

The information in this book is based on the author's experiences and opinions. The author and publisher disclaim responsibility for any adverse consequences, which may result from use of the information contained herein. Permission to use any external content has been sought by the author. Any breaches will be rectified in further editions of the book.

Cover design: Fiona Sinclair

Layout and typesetting: Busybird Publishing

Busybird Publishing
2/118 Para Road
Montmorency, Victoria
Australia 3094
www.busybird.com.au

To my father, Max Whiteside,
who introduced me to the mountains,
and would love to have lived
to see this book

Contents

Introduction		1
1	A Perilous Journey	7
2	Bill	10
3	Evelyn	13
4	Doris's Holiday	17
5	A Bright Future	21
6	Living in the Shadows	30
7	The Search for the Southern Cloud	34
8	Stoking the Fire	36
9	Homeward Bound	38
10	Rabbits in the Snow	41
11	A Train Ride Down to Melbourne	42
12	The Bombshell	47
13	The 'Charmed' Lizard	47
14	Evelyn's Return	49
15	A Tiny Hut on a Lonely Ridge	50
16	A Special Errand	53
17	A Delicate Situation	57
18	A Golden Year	60
19	A Brass Fortune?	65
20	A Cold Night (November, 1933)	66
21	A Change of Plan	68
22	An Angry, Frustrated Woman	69
23	The Elegy	73
24	Life at the Cabin	77
25	An Apartment in Melbourne	88
26	Bella	89
27	The End of the Road	91
28	Mother and Son Reunited	93
29	Bill All Alone	95
30	Fire!	97

31	Meanwhile, over at Golden Point...	100
32	Gold!	103
33	The Hard Work Begins	107
34	Struck it Rich!	112
35	A New Star in the Heavens	114
36	Table Tennis	116
37	The Nurse	118
38	A Letter from Australia	119
39	Ear Wax	122
40	And Do You Take this Man?	123
41	Another Log for the Fire	126
42	From a Hospital Bed	128
43	The Scene in Polly's Vestibule	130
44	A Messy Return	132
45	Life in the Grey Zone	138
46	Finally, a Plan	142
47	A Buyer is Found	143
A Closing Word		145
References		151
Photo credits		152
Newspapers featuring Bill's photographs		156
Captions of newspaper photographs		157
Acknowledgements		159
List of recorded interviews		162
About the Author		166
Previous books by Stephen Whiteside		167

Introduction

This book was inspired by Spargo's Hut. I first heard of it during a family skiing holiday at Mt Hotham sometime in the early 1970s. It was a fine, sunny day and a young couple staying in the same lodge as us announced that, instead of skiing on the runs that day, they were skiing out to Spargo's Hut for a picnic. I couldn't quite make out the tiny hut on the horizon, but could see the distant ridge on which it stood. It sounded like such a romantic adventure!

I first visited Spargo's Hut about ten years later, in 1982. I was bushwalking near Mt Hotham with a friend one summer, and we found ourselves a day ahead of schedule. I suggested we walk out to Spargo's Hut. When we arrived, I was shocked to discover upon looking through a window that the hut was still occupied. We ate lunch on the grass outside. I decided to look through the window again before leaving, and realised I had been mistaken. The hut was no longer occupied, but was crammed full of personal possessions, the many items of daily living. They had lain there untouched for a long time.

I became fascinated with Spargo's Hut, wondering who had lived there, and why. In 1987 I returned to the hut with a camera and several rolls of film, with the objective of performing as complete as possible a photographic inventory of its contents. Among the many items that I photographed were a table, two chairs, a bed, a pillow made from a sugar bag, a pair of boots, two home-made brooms, an overcoat, an umbrella, a home-made Coolgardie safe (to keep food cool in the days before refrigeration), pots and pans, a cheese grater, an old fly spray pump, cutlery and crockery, books and magazines, a framed painting of a sailing ship that was standing on the table, a toothbrush, a tin of buttons, a shotgun cartridge, a golf putter, a large tin of golden syrup, two big handsaws (one of which was truly enormous!), a bar of Velvet soap, a goggles case, an old oil can, an oven mitt, assorted tools, and coils of canvas hosing.

The seat of an old wooden chair had been repaired with a small steel plate. The plate was black, and upon it in white paint had been written: APPLIED FOR LEASE E. M. PIPER

Who was E. M. Piper?

I decided to find out as much as I possibly could about Bill Spargo and E. M. Piper. With the help of a few older skiers whom I knew, who were able to provide me with some initial contacts, I conducted scores of telephone interviews. I also travelled widely throughout country Victoria in 1987 and 1988 with my father's old Dictaphone microcassette tape recorder, interviewing people who had known Bill and/or Evelyn. I spoke to surviving members of Bill's family, skiing pioneers, chalet managers, prospectors and miners, cattlemen and many others. I was given photographs, private letters and other relevant documents. Gradually the story came together. I discovered that E. M. Piper was Evelyn Maud Piper, an English-born widow, who befriended, and eventually married, Bill Spargo. I also established contact with surviving members of Evelyn's family in England.

In more recent years Trove, the National Library of Australia's online digitised newspaper resource, has provided me with a large amount of further valuable information.

All the characters in this book are real people, with the exception of the skiers Doris and Clive. These are fictitious but would, I am sure, have been typical of the many young people taking to the slopes of Mt Hotham at the time. (The unnamed mother and child in Chapter 37 are also fictitious.)

I cannot tell you that everything happened exactly as I have said it did. Indeed, I am quite sure it did not. I can say, however, that I have stuck to the evidence that I uncovered, in the form of reminiscences, personal letters, other documents, and newspaper articles of the day, as much as possible. I have used my imagination, based on my reading and my discussions with others, to fill in the gaps where necessary. I have done my best to stay true to the spirit of Bill and Evelyn's story, as I perceive it to be.

I cannot say this is a love story. It has, however, been a wonderful journey of discovery, a glorious quest to solve a fascinating mystery.

I have quoted written sources directly on several occasions. Where the origins of these are not stated in the text, they can be found in the 'References' at the back of the book.

The birds we now know as currawongs were known as jays in Bill's day, and I have referred to them as jays here.

An adit is a tunnel.

My first view of Spargo's Hut.

Spargo's Hut during the winter of 1987.

This painting of a ship was standing on the table in 1987. I took it outside and placed it on the ground, resting it against the front door, to photograph it. Who painted it, and why was it in the hut?

This postcard of a red robin was standing on the mantelpiece in 1987. Bill had named his gold mine "The Red Robin."

Introduction

Who was "E. M. Piper"?

This chair probably originally came from the Chalet.

These home-made brooms were at the hut in 1987.

Coolgardie safes like these were once common throughout Australia. Relying on the principle of evaporative cooling, they kept food cool in the days before refrigeration. Lengths of cord were soaked in kerosene and wrapped around the bottoms of the legs to keep the ants away.

Maps

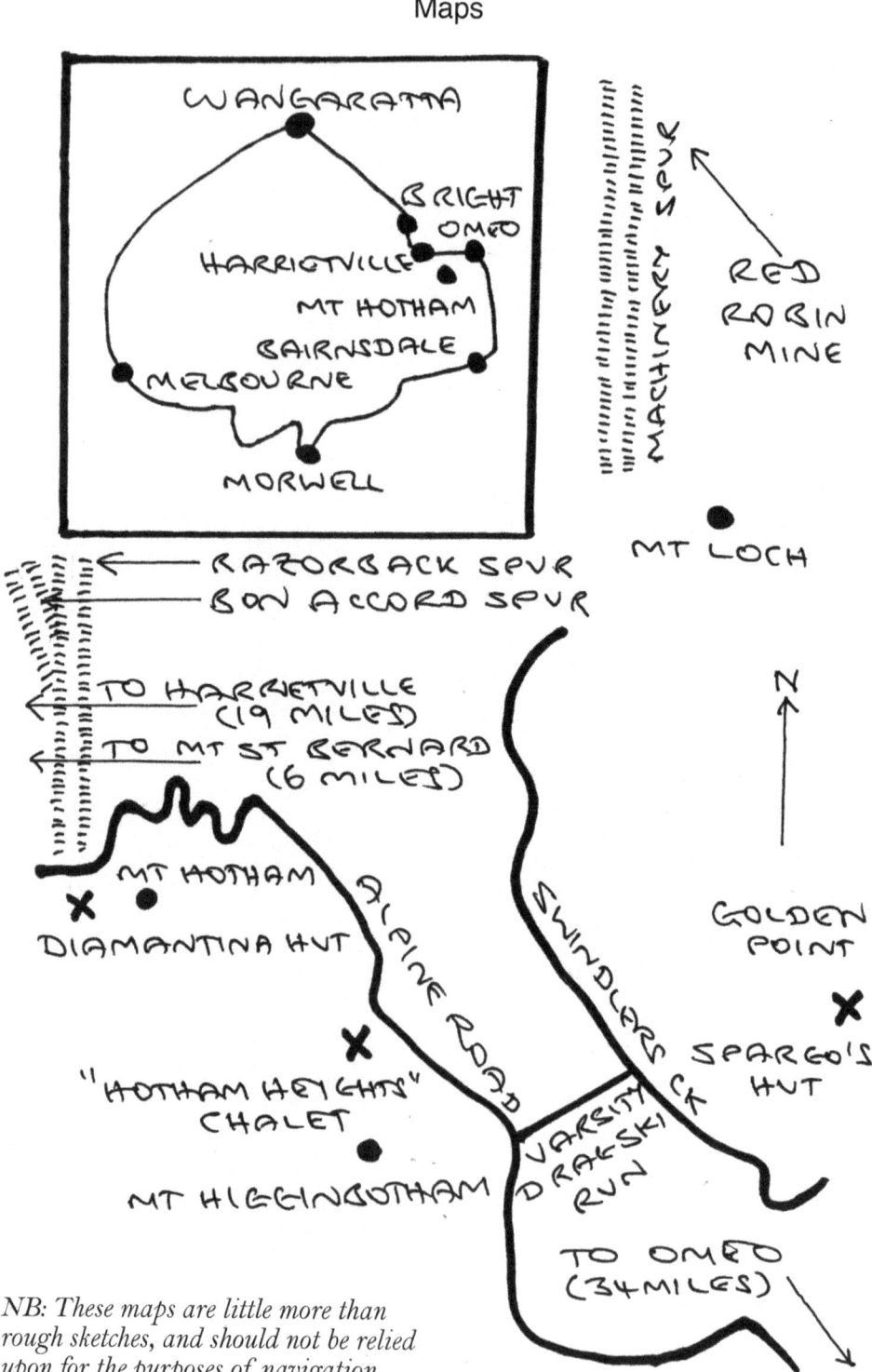

NB: *These maps are little more than rough sketches, and should not be relied upon for the purposes of navigation.*

1
A Perilous Journey

She focused her eyes on the two legs in front of her, striding determinedly through knee deep snow. Suddenly they were gone. Scrambling desperately ahead, Evelyn found Bill clinging to the edge of a rock. His thin woollen gloves offered little protection, and the tips of a couple of bleeding fingers poked through the worn material. She threw herself down onto the snow, wrapped her hands around his wrists, and pulled with all her might. Nothing. It was difficult to tell with the fog so thick all around, but the movements of his body suggested his feet were dangling in thin air. How long was the drop below?

"Let go of my left wrist!" shouted Bill above the wind.

Unthinkingly, obediently, she obeyed his order, transferring her right arm to his right forearm, where her left hand already gripped his wrist like iron. She watched as his left hand reached down to unbuckle the strap around his waist. She could see now how his backpack was pulling him down, making it impossible for him to scramble to safety. His hand returned to the rocky ledge, but she could see this final effort had exhausted him. He was tiring fast. He mumbled something, but it was so faint she could not catch it. It was obvious what she had to do, though. Letting go of his wrist, she reached forward and grabbed his pack, lifting it up and over his head. She could feel it pressing his head against the rock, but there was nothing she could do to prevent that. Suddenly, the pack came free and rolled forward, quickly coming to rest in the deep snow. She watched as Bill tried to pull himself back up and over the ridge.

The task was still beyond him. There wasn't much time now. What to do? Casting her eyes around in search of inspiration, she saw her ice stick. She lowered one end over the precipice, allowing him to grip it. Suddenly he had some leverage, and his body began to rise a little. He rested his chest briefly on the ground, and she reached down and grabbed his trouser belt where it passed behind his back. Together the two wriggled and struggled until Bill's knee reached the rock and he, too, was able to roll to safety. For a few moments, the two lay panting in the snow.

Bill regained his feet, but still stood there for a few moments, hands on knees, catching his breath. Panting, he spoke to Evelyn in a hoarse whisper:

"We're going to have to head back to Diamantina Hut. We can't make it this way."

He leant forward and grabbed his pack, throwing it back over his shoulders, and securing the waist strap once more. Evelyn nodded silently, picked up her stick, and fell into step behind him as they slowly retraced their route up the snowy slope. Trixie padded along faithfully beside them. At least now they had their footsteps to guide them. It had been 3 pm when they had left Mt Hotham, bound for the town of Harrietville in the valley below. It had seemed to her a late time to be starting such an arduous journey, particularly when the weather was so bad, but Bill's work around the Chalet was never-ending, and he was reluctant to give up any more hours of daylight. Besides, his confidence in his ability to make his way around the mountains was supreme, and she deferred to that. Now she had her doubts.

As they reached the point where the Bon Accord spur met the Razorback ridge the weather, if possible, deteriorated. They were exposed now to the full blast of the alpine gale. Snow was still falling heavily. Visibility had dropped to a couple of metres, and even their outgoing footsteps could now not be seen. Evelyn felt completely overwhelmed. There was nothing she could do. No words of advice. No offers of assistance. The world was a blur of white. It was impossible to see where the snow ended, and the fog started. Evelyn kept Bill's dark form firmly in her sight, and trudged forward, stolidly placing one foot in front of another, her mind never moving beyond the next step.

How long did they walk together like this? Ten minutes? Twenty? An hour? Suddenly she heard Bill's voice above the wind. It was not a sentence. Not even a word. Just a cry of joy. Looking up, she could see what he could see, the unmistakable black square outline of Diamantina Hut. They were safe! How had Bill found that tiny dot in this vast wilderness of snow and ice? As she later told the journalist who reported their journey, she would never know. But he had.

Bill and Evelyn stumbled through the door of the hut, too tired and cold to speak. Food was short, but there was plenty of water - or at least snow, which could be converted to water - and their lives were no longer in immediate danger. It would be another two days, the last part in the company of a search party, before they finally reached the little hamlet of Harrietville in the Ovens Valley.

Note on the back of the photo (Evelyn's hand):
"We are found by F. Wraith and Constable Anderson after 48 hours on the mountains." (photo by W. B. Spargo, courtesy Kate Piper)

2
Bill

He closed the front door gently behind him, and trudged through the crisp snow to the meteorological station. The big box sat above three concrete steps, and housed all the instruments they needed to record the weather. Readings were supposed to be taken daily, but sometimes it just wasn't possible. Today, though, they would be.

He checked the temperature. Minus six. Hard to believe with the sun high in a cloudless sky, and the glare so strong it could easily give you snow blindness if you stayed out too long without eye protection. Mind you, he had long ago found an alternative to expensive glasses or goggles. If he knew he was going to be out in the sun for any period of time, he simply blackened the skin around his eyes with charcoal from the fireplace. That seemed to do the trick.

A sudden movement to his left caught his eye. It was a jay, a glossy black bird that had likely flown up from the valley early that morning. No doubt it would soon be looking for handouts from the Chalet. It would get them, too. Outside of the ski season, it could be lonely up here. He worked hard to make friends of the animals and birds. They weren't great conversationalists, but at least they could be relied on to be fair and consistent - even loyal. That was more than could be said for several human beings he had known over the years.

Measurements taken and recorded, he began to walk back. It was such a beautiful day. He paused to look around him. He never tired of the view. To the north he could just make out the summit of Mt Feathertop, rising behind the massif of Hotham itself. Then his eyes swung around to Mt Loch, Swindlers Valley, and the

Little Plain beyond - one glorious expanse of glistening snow. He couldn't recall ever having felt so strong and secure, so confident in the future. Last year had been an absolute nightmare.

He understood that the job of running the only accommodation on the mountain for this new sport of skiing was too much for one man. He needed an assistant - a partner, even. But Helmut Kofler was not that man. It still rankled him that he had not been consulted. The Ski Club of Victoria had fallen head over heels in love with the tall, athletic, charismatic Austrian. Before he knew what had happened, he was installed beside Bill as his partner on the mountain. The skiers couldn't see what was plain to Bill. Kofler was self-centred, arrogant and inflexible. Impossible to work with. Then Kofler had given him a black eye, which he had sported for weeks. Bill had retreated from the mountain, and lived with his younger brother in Melbourne. It was the first winter in eight years he had spent away from Mt Hotham. Still, it had all worked out well in the end. Kofler now had a police record. His grand plans to develop a private resort on the mountain had been torn up and thrown in the bin, and he had skulked off to Mt Buller with his tail between his legs to try his luck there. Well, good luck to him!

Everybody knew that Hotham belonged to Bill Spargo. Hadn't he resurrected this old rocky road that led across the mountains from Omeo to Harrietville? Hadn't he been the driving force behind the construction of the new telephone line over the mountains? Hadn't he been responsible for the line of shelter huts that spread to the north and the south, making the Alps safe for travellers in all weather? And the stone Chalet itself - even that had been built for him back in the days when he was head of the road gang. No, Bill Spargo was Mt Hotham, and Mt Hotham was Bill Spargo. The two were inseparable.

Now here he was, back on his mountain, and with a partner he could work with and trust implicitly - his younger brother Cecil. Yes, it was true he and Cecil had never been close. Cecil was nine years younger, and Bill had left home as a teenager, but that year with Cecil had been good for their relationship. Now Cecil was here with him, with his wife, Nell, and their three-year-old son, Len.

Of course, they couldn't stay forever, but they had a five-year lease together, and a lot can happen in five years. Bill would hopefully be in a much more secure position by then, and able to employ a large staff.

Then there was the curious matter of this mysterious Englishwoman who had descended out of the blue with her seven-year-old son, Steven. What was he to make of her? He had never been too fussed about female company, but she was fun to be around, and he really respected the way she had handled herself during that blizzard. Let's be honest, she had probably saved his life! She seemed to like him, too. Bill chuckled to himself as he opened the door of the Chalet, and escaped from the blinding glare. Ah yes, life was good!

Picnic Point Brewery in Bairnsdale, where Bill was born.

"The Spargo Children: Polly, Bill, Cecil and Elsie"
Bill, Polly (Mary) and Elsie were all born in Bairnsdale. The youngest, Cecil, was born in Brunswick, Melbourne.

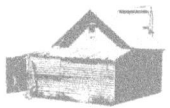

3
Evelyn

Evelyn stood at the kitchen sink, surrounded by fifty potatoes, and gazed outside. Her eye was not met by a clean white horizon against a backdrop of dazzling blue. No cloud puffs were born on the breeze. No sharp peaks rose high in the distance. No snow-covered snow gums glistened in the sunshine, and no jays called from their branches. The view, instead, was a plain sheet of white, as a three-metre-high wall of snow outside the cottage pressed against the double-glazed window.

Fifty dirty potatoes. Well, it could be worse. A lot worse. She had come here with her young son, Steven, for a holiday, but the offer had been made for board and lodging for herself and Steven if she took on the job of Bill's housekeeper at the Chalet. Why not? That was the best offer she had had for a long time. On the face of it, possibly the best ever. Life had never been easy as a young woman at the wrong end of class-ridden England. Even her childhood had been a sad, lonely affair. Her younger sister had been born prematurely, and their mother had focused most of her energies on her survival. Whatever affection and time were left over went to their brother. Males were more important than females, after all!

Things had begun to look up when she married Harry. Wonderful, loving Harry. She remembered how excited they had both been when she had fallen pregnant, but at twenty, she was young to be having a baby, and the spectre of Harry's war wound hung over them both like a black cloud. The amputation of his left arm had been a rushed job on the battlefield, and the gangrene always appeared to be one step ahead. 'Catch-up' amputation is a dreadful game, and Harry had lost it in the end. How mean the government had been! They had ruled that, because he had died after the end of the War they could not be certain that the War had caused his death, and Evelyn was therefore not eligible for the war widow's pension. Life since then had been hard indeed.

"How are you going with those potatoes? There's a cup of tea waiting for you here when you're finished!"

The call startled her out of her reverie. "Won't be long!" she stammered, thinking to herself, only forty-seven to go...

Nobody ever got too angry or tense up here. Everybody was having so much fun, you couldn't stay upset for long. The skiers had saved hard for their week or two in the snow. Nobody was going to stop them from having a good time, and their enthusiasm was infectious. Besides, there were no authority figures peering over their shoulders. If they wanted to check up on them, they could walk in the six miles over the snow. Or ten, if they'd just had a big dump.

They were a motley crew sharing this little stone house, no question about that. There were the skiers - thirty of them, all up from Melbourne, many of them university students, or just starting out in their chosen profession: doctors, lawyers, accountants, engineers and the rest. A few were the children of wealthy businessmen and appeared to have money and time on tap. Then there were the staff - a bunch of real battlers like herself. Good old Mary Johnson, the cook, had come up from Geelong. She didn't appear to have had any formal training, but had spent a lifetime raising a family and knew how to cook good, basic food. Her daughter, Gladys, was also here. In fact, if Gladys hadn't taken to bed with the flu, she would be peeling these potatoes, not Evelyn! Bill had his younger brother, Cecil, here, together with Cecil's wife and child. Len was too young to provide much companionship for Steven, though Steven was very patient with him, she noted proudly.

She herself knew little about skiing. Hardly anybody did, the sport was so new - and expensive!. With the whole mountain empty bar this one tiny building, this fragile centre of human activity, the challenges were enormous - but so was the satisfaction that came with each small success.

She was moving steadily, now, peeling these big, rough potatoes with a funny old peeler that felt a little clumsy in her hands, but was sharp enough, and did the job. The water in the sink was icy cold, and already dark brown from dirt. There wasn't much of it, either. How ironic that up here, surrounded by snow, their supply was so tenuous. Frozen and cracked pipes were a big part of the problem. Then there was the spring - unreliable at the best of times, and situated on the other side of the saddle, so that the water had to be pumped up to the top first before it could begin to flow down to them. Everything here was make-do, on the verge of complete collapse, but that was part of the adventure. Certainly the skiers thought so - though she worried sometimes that the servings of food were a little on the small side for big hearty appetites, and second helpings were a rarity indeed. She heard the occasional grumblings...let's face it, fifty potatoes weren't going to go far amongst thirty-eight hungry mouths!

Which brought her to Bill himself. What a strange fish he was. She really couldn't work him out at all. He seemed to have come from another world - a world she knew little about. Nothing ever fazed him. Ski six miles and back through a snowstorm to pick up the mail? Sure, no worries. Dig through two feet of snow and ice in the middle of the night to fix a broken pipe? Of course! Climb to the top of Mt Hotham in a howling gale to replace a length of telephone cable? Not a problem. Yet on the personal front, he was one of the shyest, most awkward men she had ever known. She was tempted to revise her earlier thoughts about everybody being easy-going up here. Bill, perhaps, was the one exception to the rule. He was so easily hurt, and he could carry that wound for days.

Yet she liked him. She didn't know why, but she did. Maybe in another place and another time the appeal would not have been so great, but up here in the mountains, it all just felt perfect. They were their own bosses, for once. There was no worry about where their next meal was coming from, and the scenery - when you could see it which, admittedly, wasn't that often - was just stunning! She could not imagine another place on Earth less like suburban London. Yes, she knew, Steven should be in school, but there was time enough for that. Life had been so, so hard. Suddenly, for the first time in her life, she found herself enjoying herself. It felt great!

"Done!" she shouted over her shoulder. "Where's that cup of tea?"

Note on the back of the photo (Evelyn's hand): "Hanging out the clothes 1930"

Evelyn standing in front of the weather station outside the Chalet. (photo by W. B. Spargo, courtesy Kate Piper)

Evelyn with her beloved Trixie. She wrote about her after their terrifying ordeal: "...faithful old Trixie who stuck to us and shared our rations and likewise the distinction with me of being the first females to cross the Alps in such a storm." (Bill had been quoted in newspaper articles saying "No other woman has ever crossed the Alps in such weather.") (photo by W. B. Spargo, courtesy Kate Piper)

4
Doris's Holiday

Doris made another attempt to get up, failed, and fell on her back again in the snow. Her legs were pointing in different directions, and her right knee hurt. Holiday? Call this a holiday? she thought to herself. She had never worked so hard in her life! Her med student boyfriend, Clive, had invited her along to enjoy this brand-new sport.

"It's all the rage!" he had bubbled to her enthusiastically. "Anybody who's anybody is doing it. It's so much fun!"

The train trip from Spencer Street Station in Melbourne to Bright had been exciting, and full of anticipation. Then they had caught a ride with one of Clive's friends who owned a motor car - so much more exciting than a horse-drawn wagon! But the snow had been heavy on the road once they had left Harrietville and started to climb through the mountains. She was told they were still a couple of miles short of St Bernard Hospice, and she knew it was a six mile walk to Mt Hotham from there, when the driver finally pulled over to the side of the road, and declared defeat. At least the weather had been fine until then, and the views most definitely glorious, but it began to turn as they took out their gear, strapped their packs to their backs, and put on their skis.

Then began the most nightmarish journey of her life as Doris, with these strange planks attached to her feet for the first time in her life, began to tentatively inch her way forward to their holiday destination. The traverse around the side of Mt Blowhard had been utterly terrifying - a sheet of solid ice, tilted at almost 45 degrees, that threatened at every step to send her sliding who knew how far down the mountain. She could barely see the person in front of her. Perhaps that was a blessing. It might have been even more frightening if she had been able to gain a full appreciation of her

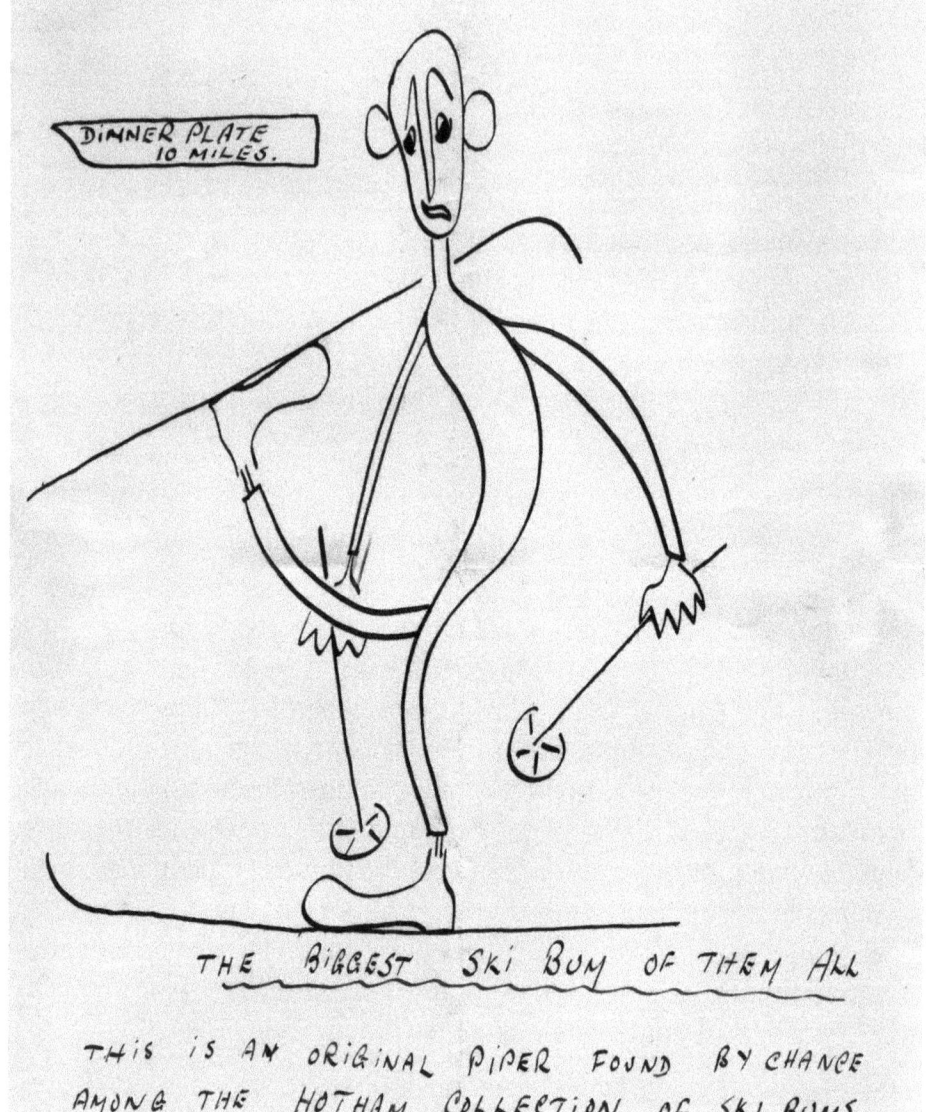

Sketch by Evelyn

Evelyn racing down a slope. (photo by W. B. Spargo, courtesy Kate Piper)

Evelyn taking a tumble. (photo by W. B. Spargo, courtesy Kate Piper)

perilous position. Then there was a long climb up over Mt Hotham, and a long trudge down the other side. Yes, there was no way she could have got down to the Chalet on skis. She had taken them off after her first, high speed, spectacular crash. She still hadn't quite forgiven Clive, either, for skiing on ahead and leaving her to make her own way down. Then, when she had finally arrived, her clothes were so frozen with ice that she couldn't remove them herself. A stranger had arrived from nowhere and untied the icy knot in the string of her cap that ran under her chin. The ear flaps were frozen solid. Then they had untied the laces of her boots for her, and helped her remove them. Talk about undignified!

With one almighty effort, Doris hauled herself to her feet, and brought her right ski back in line with her left. Oh no! She was starting to slide again. Whumph! Down she fell once more in a heap on the snow. At least it was soft, and she was warm from all the physical exertion, but if she didn't manage to free herself soon, she would no doubt start to feel the cold.

Then there was the Chalet itself. Oh my God, talk about primitive! The toilets were just big steel cans with wooden seats placed over the top. When one was full, it was simply taken out the back, and an empty one put in its place. She was told the reason the full ones didn't smell was because they were frozen solid! Water was scarce, and it was very hard to wash your hands properly afterwards.

A few lucky ones got to sleep downstairs near the big, roaring fireplace, but she and Clive were up in the attic with about twenty others. It was freezing! Siberia had nothing on it! And the food! It wasn't too bad in itself, but the servings were so small, and there were never any seconds. She had never drunk so much tomato soup in all her life, nor eaten so much bread and jam!

Ah, well. Her body wasn't going to lift itself out of the snow. Better try again, no matter how futile it appeared to be.

"There you are! I've been looking everywhere for you, you old rascal!"

It was Clive. Perhaps he wasn't so bad after all.

5
A Bright Future

Bill still struggled to believe how well things were turning out. To think, after all those bleak, early years, he could count Keith Murdoch, proprietor of The Sun newspaper, as a friend! What a thrill it was, as winter approached, and the mountains once again gained their mantle of snow, to take his own photographs, develop them himself up on the mountain, then send them down to his mate, Keith, in Melbourne, and see them printed on the front page of the paper!

He, Bill Spargo, had taken those photos! If not for him, those articles, read by half of Melbourne, would not have been written. He, Bill Spargo, was somebody! Yes, no doubt about it, he had arrived. It had taken forty years, but here he was - better late than never.

It wasn't just Murdoch, either. The lawyer Gerald Rush was also a friend. Rush had already published two of Bill's articles in the Ski Club of Victoria Yearbook - articles which served to enhance Bill's reputation, and advertise the Chalet at Hotham. He knew his spelling and punctuation left a fair bit to be desired, but Gerald was happy to look after that for him. There were many others, too - powerful friends in powerful places.

Growing up with his parents in Brunswick, all Bill had wanted to do was escape. The life of his grandfather, Benjamin, had sounded so glamorous, traipsing around northeast Victoria, sinking shafts and driving tunnels, towing batteries for crushing ore down narrow winding roads through deep forests, diverting rivers, all in the quest for that elusive metal of magic, gold! He had never quite understood why his grandfather had turned from gold mining to brewing. Perhaps he was just looking for a more peaceful life but,

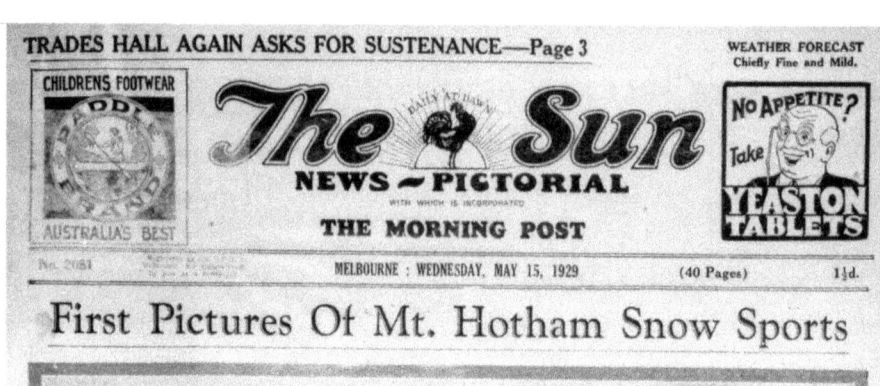

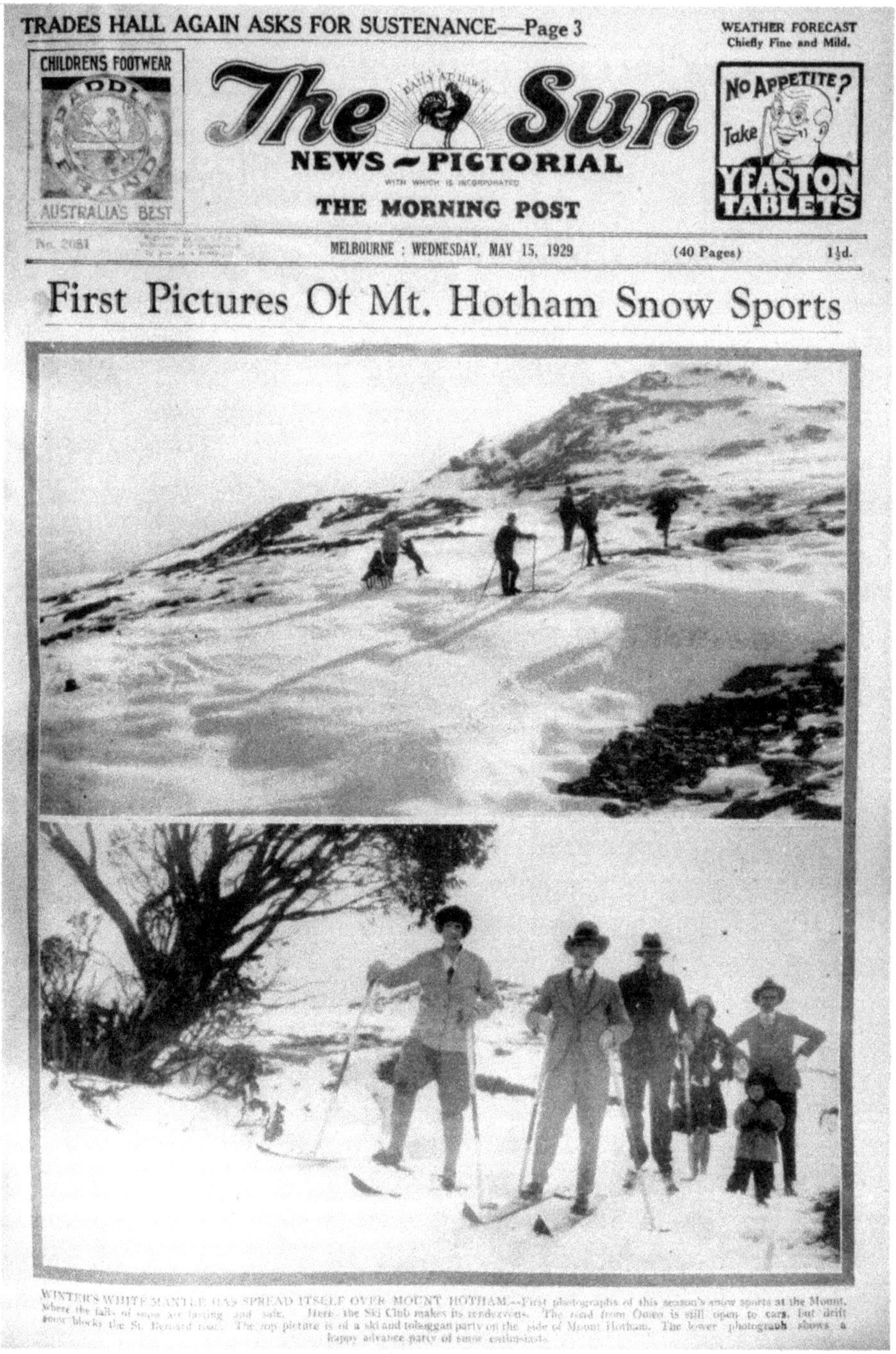

TRADES HALL AGAIN ASKS FOR SUSTENANCE—Page 3

WEATHER FORECAST
Chiefly Fine and Mild.

The Sun
DAILY AT DAWN
NEWS - PICTORIAL
WITH WHICH IS INCORPORATED
THE MORNING POST

MELBOURNE : WEDNESDAY, MAY 15, 1929 (40 Pages) 1½d.

First Pictures Of Mt. Hotham Snow Sports

WINTER'S WHITE MANTLE HAS SPREAD ITSELF OVER MOUNT HOTHAM.—First photographs of this season's snow sports at the Mount, where the falls of snow are lasting and safe. Here the Ski Club makes its rendezvous. The road from Omeo is still open to cars, but drift snow blocks the St. Bernard road. The top picture is of a ski and toboggan party on the side of Mount Hotham. The lower photograph shows a happy advance party of snow enthusiasts.

Caption can be read on page 157

A Bright Future

Captions can be read on page 157-8

Captions can be read on page 158

sadly, the venture had proved a failure. Then the Depression had come, and they had lost nearly everything. His poor mother, Bella, not long out of England, and with a small fortune in her purse, had lost it all in the service of his father's debts. His father, William, had seemed to shrink in the face of Benjamin. Yet they were both now firmly a part of him, and his identity - William Benjamin Spargo.

Then there had been that story of his grandfather killing a man in a fight. The coroner had made it clear that Benjamin was not to blame for the man's death, but the story hovered like a grey cloud over the family nonetheless, and nothing any of them could do or say ever succeeded in shifting it.

It had been touch and go in Bill's early years whether the TB would kill him. But he had looked after himself, taking cod-liver oil every day, and no doubt the clear mountain air had done its bit, too. Nowadays he felt as strong as an ox. By jeez, though, those early days working on the Hotham road had been lonely. He didn't know what he would have done without the Riggall family, down on Cobungra Station, near Omeo. It was hard to get by on the meagre Country Roads Board salary, and those big roast dinners at Cobungra Station had been a blessing, indeed. He didn't feel too guilty about it though. With all those cattle, they certainly had plenty of beef, and he had done his bit, entertaining the children - taking them on trips around the mountains in his motorbike and sidecar, and so forth. They had certainly had their fun with him - shortsheeting his bed, hiding his false teeth in the chamber pot under his bed, and all the rest of it. He didn't quite understand why he was such a ready target for teasing, but it was all in good fun, and they had grown very fond of each other. Singing together around the piano had been an especial joy.

Even up here at Hotham, though, he found it hard to exert authority. Sometimes the skiers failed to give him the respect he felt that he was due. It was hard to get them to go to bed at a reasonable time, for instance. The noise would keep everybody awake, and they all would be a bit grumpy the next day. And one of them had cheekily nailed a sardine can to the wall, with the inscription 'Rations' beneath it. That was a bit rough! He did his best. It wasn't easy getting food into Hotham - pretty much impossible once the winter had set in - and it wasn't cheap, either. He'd tried borrowing from the banks in the past, but they weren't prepared to offer anything. What did people expect? They really had no right to complain. The mountains were now safer than they had ever been.

Best of all, Bill was sure there was gold around here. Indeed, he had already found a little. What more noble pursuit could there be than the search for gold? For the sake of his grandfather, and the family name, he would find it. One way or another he, William Benjamin Spargo, would find gold!

"Cecil Spargo 100 Wilson Street, Brunswick" Cecil standing outside the Spargo family home.

This is one of six portraits of Bill that appear to have been taken in a studio.

I do not know where "Evelyn Falls" are.

HOTHAM HEIGHTS IN WINTER.   EXCLUSIVE SERIES.

"My favourite picture of Hotham Heights. WBS" (Bill's hand)

"Hotham Heights" chalet in summer.

Members of the Melbourne Walking Club relax in the lounge room of the Chalet.

"A party of ski-ers at Hotham in August 1929" (Evelyn's hand)

Note on the back of the photo: (Bill's hand)
"Snow drifts intersect the Alpine Rd in summer months. The snow is frozen hard and explosives have to be used to shift it. Vic Alps. The altitude at this point is over 6200 ft. WBS"

Bill's motorcycle

"The Edge of Beyond" (Evelyn's hand)

6
Living in the Shadows

Evelyn smiled as little Len leapt out from under yet another dinner table, frightening yet another bunch of guests with his toy crocodile. It was beautifully crafted, built by his father, Cecil, who was so good with his hands. The attention to detail was marvellous, with the teeth bright white and the tongue deep red. Len was a lovely boy. That, too, could not be denied. Yet she felt frustrated - resentful even - that once again her own son, Steven, was pushed out of the limelight. Steven had no father to make him a toy crocodile. Steven was too old to compete with Len for cuteness, and was not the nephew of Bill, the man in charge.

Then there had been the whole business of the trip to Omeo. Cecil had picked up a job doing some work on a house there. It was August and he decided to ski there with Len. In her own mind it had been a foolhardy venture, but they had picked the weather well, and it had made a big splash. The papers loved it. They had actually skied less than half that distance, but nobody was going to quibble about that. No matter how you looked at it, it was a great achievement. Once again, it was Len front and centre, and Steven nowhere to be seen.

Evelyn felt as though it had been like that all of Steven's life. it was so unfair. It would have all been so different if Harry had lived. They probably never even would have come to Australia - certainly not now, with Steven so young. They would have been living in substantial comfort somewhere in England, probably London. Steven would have had a sibling by now, maybe two. Was she idolising Harry, she wondered, now that he was dead? Were cracks in the relationship beginning to emerge, that she was now denying? No, she honestly didn't think so. They had adored each other. It was just that wretched war that had ruined everything.

THREE YEAR OLD SKI EXPERT

This is Leonard Spargo, aged 3, whose home is higher than any other boys in Australia. He lives 6000 feet above sea level, and has become, under the tutorage of his uncle, Mr W. B. Spargo, an expert ski runner.

The Herald, Tuesday July 30 1929, page 1

It had been sickening to discover just how reduced were her circumstances following Harry's death. No inheritance or income of any sort had fallen to her at all. Nothing. Doodly-squat. She had been forced entirely on to her own resources to support herself and her young child. Her parents had been able to help a little, but they were not rich. She had felt, too, the frustrations of being tied down while still in her early twenties. Work as a cleaner for the local school had been followed by a job in a department store. Neither of these offered much for a young woman with an independent nature and a free spirit. Moreover, these jobs relied on her posing as a single woman, denying the very existence of her son. That is why the prospect of travelling the world, with Steven beside her, had been so attractive. A man with more money than sense, whose wife had left him, had advertised for a governess to escort him and care for his daughter during their international travels. Evelyn had grabbed the opportunity with both hands. Could she bring her own son with her? Yes, that shouldn't be a problem, provided she was reasonably discreet about it. The start of Steven's life in the shadows...

It hadn't turned out quite as she had hoped. The man was a drunk, a conman, a lecher. He needed to keep moving, to stay ahead of his past. She had tolerated it for a while. Shipboard life agreed with her, with all its little diversions and amusements. The legacy of her grandfather's talent as the designer and manufacturer of uniforms had come in handy. She had even won a dressmaking competition! But eventually she could stomach it no more and had washed up on the shores of Australia.

Now here they were, holed up in this tiny stone cottage, the only accommodation on one of the highest and most remote mountains in the state of Victoria. If there was a better place to hide from the harshness of the world, she could not think of it. Yet this was no paradise. She was working very hard every day, and Bill's brother and wife only really tolerated them rather than truly accepting and welcoming them. Bill wanted her here, though, and she wanted Steven here, and for now, that was enough.

Steven with the dogs

Bill and Steven

Note on the back of the photo (Evelyn's hand):
"The Young Geologist 1930"

7
The Search for the Southern Cloud

The news reports were full of it. The Southern Cloud, an aeroplane carrying six passengers and two crew on a commercial flight from Sydney to Melbourne, had gone missing. The weather had been bad, and the worst was feared. Reports from the nearby towns of Eskdale and Tallangatta suggested it may have crashed nearby.

Bill stood at the top of the saddle between Mts Hotham and Higginbotham, and strained his eyes to the southwest. Two large white objects on the slopes of Mt Howitt looked suspiciously like aeroplane wings. It would take him a week to walk there himself. He returned to the Chalet, and rang the Omeo police station. Apparently he was not the only person to be concerned. Constable McMillan, currently out on patrol quite near Mt Howitt, had also spotted them.

*

The following day, Bill was joined by Inspector Barber from Bairnsdale. They stood side by side at the top of the saddle. Bill shifted restlessly from foot to foot as the inspector trained his powerful telescope directly at the large white objects.

"Can you see them?" he asked anxiously.

"Yep," replied the inspector calmly after a short delay.

"And...?"

"Definitely not wings, Bill. No. They're just big drifts of snow."

"Are you sure?"

"Yes. Look for yourself."

Bill peered down the narrow eyepiece. It took him a while to adjust his focus.

"Well I'll be blowed!"

Deep snow drifts in March! Bill was shocked!

8
Stoking the Fire

Some men are born into a trade. A lucky few are born into a profession. Bill Spargo was not one of these men. He was, however, acutely aware that there was a strong family tradition of mining - prospecting first, and then, if you are lucky, mining the rich deposit that you have found. Prospecting is a bit like the entertainment industry - most make little if anything, but a tiny few make fabulous fortunes.

Benjamin Spargo had come over to Australia as a young man, with his brother and father, from the copper mining county of Cornwall in England. A brief stint at copper mining in South Australia had not proved productive, and he had moved to the famous goldfields of central Victoria. Here the competition was intense, however, and he moved once again, this time to the less spectacular, less famous, but nonetheless quite promising goldfields in the elevated, remote country of northeast Victoria.

Any inheritance that had survived the 1890s Depression had been divided between his thirteen offspring, of whom William John Spargo, Bill's father, was one. Bill had left the struggling Melbourne home as soon as he could, to begin afresh the family's search for gold. He had inherited the passion and the drive, if not the financial rewards. An early stint working for others at the Mt Wills goldfield, snowbound in winter, had been a great experience, but was not what he was looking for. He wanted the challenge and the satisfaction of finding his own gold deposit. Time spent working on the Tallangatta-Omeo Road between Glen Wills and Granite Flat, Benjamin's old stamping ground, had allowed him to keep the wolf from the door while paying tribute to his grandfather's legacy.

The hydraulic sluicing operations of the Cobungra Gold Mining Company at the Brandy Creek gold mine, only a short distance south of Mt Hotham, had captured Bill's imagination during his days working on the Alpine Road. An ancient stream bed, containing significant deposits of gold had, millions of years ago, been covered by volcanic rock. This 'overburden' had first to be removed before the gold in the 'deep lead' could be reached. Water diverted via a man-made channel from a nearby stream could then be passed through a series of pipes, each one narrower than the last, until the water finally emerged from the nozzle in such a narrow, fast powerful jet that the worthless basalt could easily be blasted away, revealing the treasure that lay beneath.

Its full significance caught him by surprise. Standing one day at the edge of the J. B. Plain, and looking to the north, he saw that two saddles, almost identical in outline and altitude, lined up perfectly, one in front of the other. Surely....surely, this must be a remnant of the ancient stream bed being worked so successfully at Brandy Creek. A fire was started. A dream was born. If Bill could find a northern continuation of the Brandy Creek deep lead system close to the slopes of Mt Hotham, the sense of satisfaction and achievement would be immense. The discovery of gold would be wonderful in its own right, of course, but this would mean so much more than that. This would be an intellectual achievement, also. It would mark Bill not only as a superb bushman and prospector but also as a deep thinker, a man who understands the world around him, and a man who had the courage of his convictions, who took the longer view. Perhaps most importantly of all, it would mark Bill to himself as a man worthy of carrying the name of Spargo. It might even go some way to rehabilitate the family name in the minds of others, removing the grey cloud that had always hung over them.

Bill loved the mountains in the winter. He appreciated their beauty, the isolation suited him, and he revelled in the challenge of living successfully in such a hostile environment. But as the warmer months arrived once more, as the snow began to thin on the northern slopes and patches of grass began to show through, as the creeks began to roar, filled with sparking snow melt, his pulse began to quicken. The prospecting season was arriving again!

9
Homeward Bound

Shipboard life agreed with Evelyn. The ocean soothed her, just as did the mountains. They were both so far removed from civilised life, from the narrow constricting norms of society. True, there were many people on this ship, but they were all touched by freedom, were a little less inhibited than they otherwise might be - a bit like the skiers at Mt Hotham. The usual rules did not quite apply. Taboos could be bent a little, if not entirely broken.

Once again, as in the mountains, the birds caught her attention. They were different birds of course, but birds were birds - beautiful, powerful, carefree, in control of their destiny (or so it appeared), completely indifferent to the fortunes of Man, arrogant even. In a way, Bill was the closest person she had ever known to a bird. He shared their resilience, their ingenuity, their ability to survive under the most adverse conditions. He relied on nothing more than his bare hands, his natural courage and his native wits. He read the weather like nobody she had ever known. He had saved so many people who had found themselves confounded by the folds in the hills, the low temperatures, the high winds and the poor visibility. Bill was always the first person the police turned to when a party was reported lost. He survived on the barest of food, the barest of clothing, the barest of shelter. It was a model to aspire to - an independence from the people who would hold her down, judge her, try to push her into places she didn't want to be. Money, class and gender mattered so much less in the mountains, and it was like that on a ship to some extent, too.

Bill was nothing like Harry, of course. It was hard to see how she could be so strongly attracted to two such different men. If Harry had lived, he would have protected her from all that she now felt she needed to be protected from. Then again, if Harry had not died, she might never have discovered this whole other side to her personality - this yearning for freedom, and the wild places of the world. It would have been a safer life, a happier life perhaps, but also less adventurous, less spectacular, less dangerous. Had Harry done her a favour? Who knew? How to judge?

Her daydreams were interrupted by the arrival of Steven at the rail beside her. Harry's death had done poor Steven no favours, that much she was sure of - deprived of a father, and now almost deprived of a mother. It had been wonderful sharing those few years with him at Hotham, but the clock was ticking. He needed an education. Already, he had fallen far behind. He was a smart boy, though, and Evelyn was confident he would catch up quickly. If only she had some family in Australia, she could have left him with them. There were good schools in Albury. She could have visited him there every couple of weeks, at least in the snow-free months. But no. That was not an option. Back to England, and his grandparents, it had to be. He didn't want to live with them, and without her. He had made that clear. It was a terrible choice to have to make. Stay with her son, her one and only child, in dull, stuffy, England, and say goodbye to the glorious times with Bill Spargo at Mt Hotham, or return to the life she loved, and say goodbye to Steven? It was not a permanent parting, of course, but exactly how long it would be, neither one could tell.

It was Bill's confidence in his future at Hotham that had turned the tide for her. He had offered to place her role as housekeeper at the Chalet on a much more secure and formal footing. It would no longer be simply a matter of paying for food and board. She would now be on a good salary. This would go a long way towards paying Steven's school fees. They would be a constant struggle for her parents otherwise, and she wished to relieve them of that as much as possible. Then there were Bill's dreams of finding gold. She knew how few prospectors truly 'struck it rich', but Bill's faith in his own ability was so strong, it was impossible not to believe in him. Perhaps one day she would share in a fortune beyond her wildest dreams... Yet still her heart was broken. Would Steven ever forgive her? Would she ever forgive herself? So many people were quick to judge, to call her a bad mother, an evil woman, even. Well, they could think what they liked. She had to harden herself against that sort of rubbish, or she would go nowhere, and do nothing. Her parents, bless their souls, had told her they would support whatever decision she made, though she could see she was something of a puzzle to them, too, and that they worried about her future.

Evelyn pressed herself close against Steven, and put her arm around his shoulder. For now, they were together, and it was important that these last few precious days not be spoiled by doubt and recriminations. They gazed at a nearby albatross, watching with admiration as it soared above the waves, and then dropped down towards them, skimming the water with a wing tip before rising once more to repeat the same, glorious cycle forever.

10
Rabbits in the Snow

Bill paused in his work, sawing the branches off a snow gum. The temperature was at freezing point, but the sweat was dripping off him. There was still much work to do if the Drag run was to be ready for the skiers when they arrived for their championships next month, and fine days like these were pure gold. He could not afford to waste any of them. Even though it was late in the day, he pushed himself to keep going, and make the most of the fading light.

A flash of movement to the left caught his eye. He turned his head. Rabbits! They were everywhere these days. They appeared not to be afraid of him in the least, and there seemed to be more every year. The snow obviously didn't worry them, either. These were doing something he had never seen before, though. If he was not mistaken, they were eating gumnuts.

He had long noticed that the rabbits remained in their burrows over the winter. As the snow covered their entrances, they would simply dig through it to the surface. Their footprints were everywhere. Sometimes they had to burrow as much as ten feet through the snow. But what were they eating? All their usual food was also well and truly buried.

He had also noticed that gang-gang cockatoos flew up to the mountains every day to eat the gumnuts from the trees, shaking the branches violently. Many nuts lay uneaten on the ground. This, then, must be the key to the puzzle. The rabbits were eating the gumnuts that the cockatoos had shaken from the trees! It would make a good story for the papers - a quirky way to help promote Mt Hotham and the upcoming skiing championships. He made a mental note to contact a journalist, and returned to his sawing.

11
A Train Ride Down to Melbourne

Bill had plenty of time to reflect during the train trip down to Melbourne from Bright in December 1932. The gum trees whipped past his window. Each one took him further away from his beloved home, the mountains, towards the alien-feeling and, to his mind, inferior environment of the busy city. He had built a reputation now. He was becoming a man of substance, a public identity who stood for something other than the rush of people to and from office blocks. Had The Herald not published a magnificent article featuring him and his philosophy in the 'Magazine Section' of its Saturday evening edition, back in June? He had poured everything he could into that article. It was a culmination of all his most memorable experiences in the mountains, together with the lessons he had learnt. It had stamped him in the public mind as a strong, interesting, if somewhat unusual personality. No doubt he would be greeted by the press upon his arrival at Spencer Street. He would tell them that the city's tall buildings struck him as small and insignificant compared to the grandeur of nature in his mountain home.

What an exciting whirlwind of a year it had been! Admittedly, it had got off to a shaky start. Evelyn had sent him a Christmas card last year, and then several months had gone by before he had heard from her again. Thinking back on it now, it was shocking how quickly his mental state had deteriorated. Had she fallen ill, or been victim to an accident? Had her feelings for him cooled now that she was back in more familiar surroundings, and in the bosom of her family? Whatever the reason, life without Evelyn was unthinkable. None of this - the snow, the mountain, the Chalet... even the gold - meant anything without Evelyn by his side. The low point had been when a letter from his aunt arrived, and he had opened it expecting it to be from Evelyn. Eventually, though, Evelyn's letter had arrived, and everything had been restored to its rightful order. He had been able to turn his full attention once more to the dramatic events taking place around him.

Hotham - his Hotham - had hosted the first ever National Skiing Championships. It had been the first time Victoria had competed directly against New South Wales. They had even had some observers from Tasmania. The races had achieved a huge amount of publicity - all of it positive. The event had also centred attention on his ski run, the Varsity Drag, now known across the breadth of the land as the nation's steepest!

Wonderful though it all had been, it was time now to take the next big step forward. It was time to further consolidate his position as host of the skiers and other paying guests, and also step up his prospecting activities. He would apply for a small parcel of Crown Land down on that flat land at the bottom of the Drag, beside Swindlers Creek, where Kofler had planned to situate his ornamental lake. It was a perfect location for a guest house - quiet and secluded, and out of the wind. It did not offer the spectacular views of the Chalet, but it had the creek! It offered excellent fishing, and swimming was not out of the question during the summer months. With a bit of luck, he could even grow a bit of a garden there. True, the walk in and out, down and back up the Drag, would be a challenge, but they were a hardy lot who chose to take their holidays in the mountains, and he could always help them with their gear. Could it operate during the winter months also? That was an interesting question. The skiers would have to look after themselves. He couldn't be in two places at once. They would need to ski in and walk out carrying their suitcases. That would be tough! It might be possible, though...

But that was not all. He was sure there was a deep lead somewhere around the Little Plains, at the end of that long ridge on the opposite side of Swindlers Valley. Its very name was encouraging - Golden Point! It was just a matter of driving an adit into the hillside at the right place. He would employ a couple of men to do the work. You needed at least two men for a job like that - one to hold the hammer, and the other to hold the drill, and turn it as the hammer struck. He couldn't work on it himself. His duties at the Chalet prevented that, but at least he would be able to supervise them closely. Besides, he didn't have the experience required for such hard rock mining. If the walls and roof were not timbered properly, the whole thing could fall in.

Once he had taken out his Miner's Right, of course, he would be entitled to build himself some accommodation. That little plateau at the southern end of the Little Plains looked like the perfect place for a small cabin. Indeed, he had already begun to cart building materials out to the site. It was a very rocky road - difficult, but manageable. Bill's pulse quickened as his plans took shape in his mind.

Soon Evelyn would be back by his side once more. How sweet it would be to have her with him to share in all the adventures and triumphs that lay ahead for them both! After all those years of loneliness and back-breaking labour, everything was finally starting to come together!

Bill felt the train slowing down. It whistled loudly as it pulled into the station. He stood and reached for his portmanteau and umbrella, both resting on the rack above his head. His heart pounded in his chest!

Note on the back of the photo (Bill's hand):
"On the Rocky Road to Little Plains Summer 1932"
The area near what is now known as "Golden Point", where Spargo's Hut stands, was once known as "Little Plains." This photograph constitutes the only clear evidence I have seen of when construction of the hut began.

12
The Bombshell

Bill submitted his application for three acres of Crown Land beside Swindlers Creek for a garden and residence to the Under Secretary for Lands. Acutely aware of the limitations of his own writing skills, he arranged for somebody else to write it, and added his signature at the bottom. It was dated 15th December 1932. The application was met with alarm and dealt with as a matter of urgency. On the face of it, there was no good reason why Bill's application should be refused. The area in question had been classified as pastoral - for the use of grazing cattle - and was free for occupation. However, a recommendation that 320 acres of land, including the land that Bill was requesting, "be exempted from occupation or business under any miner's right or business licence" was drawn up quickly, and signed by the Under Secretary for Lands on 22nd December.

The application was further discussed with the Mines Department, who referred it to the Country Roads Board. On 18th February 1933, the Secretary of the Country Roads Board wrote the following to the Under Secretary for Lands.

Regarding the application of W. B. Spargo, the Board desires to reiterate the views expressed by it in connection with a similar request made by H. Kofler.

The Board visited Hotham Heights this week and has decided to terminate Spargo's lease for CRB cottage.

He appears to devote the whole of his time to mining operations to the neglect of the business of catering for tourists for which his lease was granted.

In addition, the Board is now convinced that Spargo is not competent or suitable for managing a business of this character.

On 27th February 1933 the Under Secretary for Lands wrote the following letter, addressed to 'Mr. W. B. Spargo, <u>HOTHAM HEIGHTS</u>'.

Sir,

With further reference to your application to have 3 acres of Crown Lands in the parish of Hotham made available for selection as a site for a garden and residence, I have to inform you that owing to an objection lodged by the Country Roads Board your request has been refused.

An area of 320 acres in the parishes of Hotham and Yertoo has been excepted, by Order in Council, from occupation for residence or business under any Miner's Right or Business licence.

Yours obediently,

Under Secretary for Lands.

Handwritten notes at the bottom suggest that Bill received official notification sometime in March 1933.

Management of the Hotham Heights Chalet transferred from the Country Roads Board to the Victorian Railways, who already managed the Chalet at Mt Buffalo and the Bungalow at Mt Feathertop, in time for the 1933 ski season.

13
The 'Charmed' Lizard

Nell answered the door. The man standing on the doorstep introduced himself as a journalist from The Herald newspaper. Normally, she would call for Bill in a situation like this, but he was in no mood to talk to the press. Besides, he and Cecil were a long way from the Chalet, far away at Golden Point. She would have to manage without them.

What to tell him, though? Why was he here? Was he simply trying to rub Bill's nose in his own grief, to give the public some titillating misery? Well, she wasn't going to give him any satisfaction, that much she knew for sure. Distraction, that was the key. She needed to give the journalist something that was more interesting, more unusual than anything that was already on his mind. Her brain racing at a hundred miles an hour, she invited him in for a cup of tea, taking his hat and coat and placing them on the rack by the front door.

Nell found herself prattling in a panicked way as she poured the water into the kettle and tipped a few spoonsful of tea into the pot. So much had happened - was continuing to happen - in the last few months. It was of immense interest to them, but none of it, surely, would be of any interest to this newspaperman. He would see it all as utterly trivial. They had cleared the plateau, erected the tent, commenced the construction of the cabin. All of this was now critical to Bill's life and future, but none of it was of any wider interest. The bored look on the journalist's face confirmed her suspicions, too. This was going badly. She had that sinking feeling.

She was becoming more and more desperate, searching around for little stories to offer this news-hungry suited man from Melbourne. She found herself talking about the little frill-necked lizard, the water dragon, that had wandered into the tent and found itself transfixed by her mouth organ playing. The journalist was transfixed, too. Was this the story that was going to save them? She explained how the lizard raised its head and front legs, spread out wide, when anyone spoke. As soon as she started playing, it approached her. No matter whether the tune was fast or slow, the lizard responded in a positive way to the music. Eyes gleaming, the journalist bolted down his tea, shook her hand vigorously, and beat a rapid retreat down the mountain. Presumably he now had what he wanted!

14
Evelyn's Return

Evelyn stood at the handrail, with countless others, waving goodbye to Steven and her parents. The great ship gradually pulled away from the wharf. She waited there a long time, but eventually individual figures could no longer be made out. Her eyes still streaming with tears, she finally turned away.

She felt sick. Had she made the right decision? Australia was so far away. The journey was so long, and so expensive. Each trip was a major undertaking. When would she be returning? Would she ever return? Steven had reacted so calmly to the news that she was returning to Bill, it unnerved her. Did he truly accept her decision so easily? He was a sensitive, intelligent boy. Had it been an act, designed to protect the feelings of his mother? Or did he simply realise that protest was futile? Was he simply resigned to his fate?

Was she a bad mother? How could she do this? she asked herself. She had only one child. That child had only one parent. Harry's parents had never been very involved in Steven's care, but fortunately, her own parents were wonderful. They loved Steven dearly, and she knew he loved them, too. The pull of Australia, those glorious mountains, and that crazy man who lived in them, was just too strong. The choice was so stark. There was no middle ground. Either she accept a life of eternal drudgery in England, or she pick up her life of adventure in Australia where she had last left it. Pull at her heartstrings as it inevitably did, there was really no choice.

Seagulls squawked fiercely above her, searching for scraps of food. She looked forward to crossing the equator, and seeing those beautiful albatrosses again.

15
A Tiny Hut on a Lonely Ridge

Bill winced as he stumbled for the umpteenth time. The table was heavy, and awkward to carry. The horse and cart had taken them as far as the pole line - and that had been wild enough - but they'd been on their own since then. The ground was uneven underfoot, and he often found himself thrust suddenly forward, and struggling to find a secure footing. Cecil, walking behind, was doing his best to match Bill's tempo, but he was unable to even see his feet. It was hard to know who had the worst of it. The snow gums snagged the table, and sometimes whipped across their faces. Then there were the fallen trees they had to scramble over as best they could.

Cecil could have fashioned a dining room table on site at the cabin, that was true. It certainly would have been much easier than carrying one over to the hut intact. Cecil was a very accomplished tradesman, no question, but there was no way he could have made a proper, cosy, slightly ornamental dining room table out there in the bush. Only another ten - maybe fifteen - minutes to go, and they would have it safely ensconced in its new home.

It was exciting to finally have his own base. It was modest, but it was his. Back at the Chalet there were always other people to think about, competing priorities, skiers and other tourists - and staff - with needs and demands that had to be met. Out here, he was his own boss. It took him two hours' hard walking through steep, trackless bush to get here from the Chalet, so if anybody wanted to follow him, well, good luck to them! Even back in the 19th century, gold had been found here - not a lot, admittedly, but the old miners lacked Bill's determination, persistence and talent. (That's what he told himself, anyway.) They probably hadn't noticed those two saddles lining up at the J B Plain, either. They hadn't seen this vital clue to the northern continuation of the Brandy Creek deep lead system.

The pressure had been on from the very beginning. He knew he'd be given a couple of months' grace, but they would have to be out of the Chalet well before the onset of winter to allow the new managers time to move in and make their preparations. If they didn't get this cabin built before the snow season, Bill would have to leave the mountains. Then there was the question of Evelyn. He felt sick about Evelyn. She was somewhere out in the Indian Ocean, making her way dreamily to an exciting future in Australia, oblivious to the fate that really awaited her. Could he have warned her? Should he have warned her?

It had been a hell of a job getting this far. First, they had had to clear the thick bush on the plateau itself. It was a fire hazard as it stood, and they needed to get rid of as much of it as possible. It wasn't a job he would have tackled with any enthusiasm by himself, but having Cecil there with him made all the difference. This whole venture at Hotham with Cecil and his family was like a new start for them both. They were really, finally getting to know each other for the first time. Nell was a bit on the bossy side, that was for sure. He was glad he wasn't married to her, and couldn't quite understand why Cecil was, but he seemed to be happy enough - or perhaps he was just resigned to his fate. If she kept Cecil on the straight and narrow, and didn't interfere with Bill's own plans, which she didn't, then he couldn't ask for more than that.

There had been one unfortunate incident during the clearing of the bush, but events like that were unavoidable, really. A red robin had been forced out of a bush they were chopping down, and come to rest temporarily on the exposed branch of a dead gum tree. A sparrowhawk had pounced upon it immediately. It was such a shame to hear the little bird's futile cries of distress. Still, perhaps they were lucky it had only happened once.

Carrying the long sheets of corrugated iron in on their backs had been thankless work, too. Many people had said he was crazy to build in such an inaccessible, isolated site, but he couldn't see what all the fuss was about. People were soft, there were no two ways about it. There had been a real sense of camaraderie when the four of them had lived in that old army tent while the cabin was being built. Bill had moved into the cabin as soon as it was vaguely habitable, leaving the family to some privacy.

There was a natural spring only a few yards away, too. It was very handy having such a reliable water supply 'on tap' as it were. Bill had plans to divert some of the water directly to the cabin. What could be more convenient than that? That water might even save his life one day!

The position was all he could hope for - remote, yet with wonderful views. The ground fell away steeply on three sides. To the east lay the valley of the Cobungra River, with the Bogong High Plains rising behind. To the west lay the valley of Swindlers Creek, with the Hotham ski runs on the far side, and the whole of Swindlers Valley opening up to the north. That deep lead system was so close he could almost taste it!

The only thing missing was Evelyn. He would love to have been able to share these times with her, and the presence of Nell and Len only served to accentuate her absence. Still, Bill was by nature a loner. He was used to living by himself. In a way, it surprised and puzzled him that he felt so deeply for a woman. He had never expected to. Besides, she wouldn't be away long. She had promised him that. She would be back to join him at the Chalet as soon as possible.

Another couple of grunts, and the table was finally in place against the wall of the cabin, beneath the two beautiful windows that Cecil had so expertly crafted. He lifted the billy off the fire that Nell had stoked in their absence, and threw in a handful of tea leaves. A couple of minutes later, he poured the hot tea into two old mugs as they sat handsomely on the smooth surface of the table's top, and leant back luxuriantly into a chair. So much work lay ahead of him, but for now, it felt right to relax for a few minutes, and reflect on all that had been achieved so far.

16
A Special Errand

Bill sat in the driver's seat of the old truck, and turned the key in the ignition. The engine kicked into life after a few turns of the starter motor. That was a relief. It had been lying idle for a couple of months now. He eased the old beast out onto the road. There had been a light fall of snow overnight, and patches remained on the ground. It was a bit late in the season to be embarking on a trip like this, but the timing had been out of his control.

There was a short climb before the long descent to Harrietville, and he wondered if the cold engine would cope. The mountain was so quiet now that Cecil and his family had decamped to Mt Buffalo. A jay eyed him from the branch of a snow gum as he passed it by. Cecil had been offered a contract to build safety fencing around the top of the gorge, and it would have been crazy not to have accepted it. The cabin had proved itself weatherproof, and the principal remaining task was to chop enough wood for the winter. Early indications were that the little stove did a good job of keeping the room warm, but the real challenge would come in winter, when the plateau was likely to be blanketed with six feet or more of snow.

The engine chugged away happily enough. It was all downhill from here - until the return journey, of course. The truck was really far too big for a trip like this. The only alternative, though, was his motor bike and sidecar, and there would be nowhere for Evelyn to put her suitcases. There was not much sign of life as he passed the Hospice at Mt St Bernard, but there was smoke coming out of the chimney, and he glimpsed a couple of grazing goats.

Evelyn was waiting patiently outside the gate when he reached the railway station at Bright. Two suitcases stood on the ground beside her, one on either side. It was wonderful to see her smiling face again. It had been nearly a year. When should he tell her? And how? Should he blab it out as soon as she plonked herself down on the seat beside him, or wait until they were back at Hotham? He gave her a quick hug, then grabbed the two suitcases, one by one, and tossed them up onto the tray of the truck. The drive to Harrietville was spent recounting her trip back from England, which had all gone smoothly enough.

The steep climb began abruptly immediately they left the little town, and the road swung sharply to the left. Bill threw the truck into first gear. Now seemed like the right time, though he had to shout to be heard above the roar of the engine.

"I've been sacked!"

"What?"

A little louder: "I've been sacked!"

"Did you say you've been sacked?"

Bill nodded.

"What do you mean?"

So out it all came. The sense of confidence that had built in Bill during a ski season like no other. The concerns about Bill's catering, and the lack of discipline amongst the guests, that had persisted in spite of this. The overarching ambition of the Victorian Railways to run the state's burgeoning skiing industry, and as much of the rest of its tourism as possible. And above it all, the apparent anger and frustration at the high priority that Bill placed upon his gold-seeking activities.

Evelyn was shocked, but not entirely surprised. She sat silently, asking no questions, trying to take it all in. When Bill had finished, she continued to remain silent for some time. Bill was heaving with the combined effort of wrestling with the truck's ancient gear box while trying to make himself heard above the roar of the engine. He glanced nervously to his left, to see a tear making its way down her cheek.

Eventually she spoke.

"So what happens to us?"

"We'll have to live in the cabin."

"But weren't you planning to build that out at the end of Little Plain?"

"Yes, that's right."

"High up on that little plateau on the far side of Swindlers Creek?"

Bill nodded.

"Oh my God! So we'll be living there?"

Bill paused a little before replying.

"It's not so bad once you get used to it," he then offered, a little nervously. "It takes me about two hours from Hotham."

"Down one steep slope and up another. Through trackless bush. Assuming you don't get lost."

"I don't get lost."

"YOU don't get lost. What about me?"

Bill said nothing.

"How long will it take with deep snow on the ground?"

Bill took a deep breath before replying again.

"I don't know. I've never tried."

Evelyn paused this time.

"It's a single room hut, right?"

Bill nodded again.

"Is there a toilet?"

Bill hesitated. "Yes." Another pause: "It's a bit rough."

Evelyn stared at Bill in disbelief. She was beyond anger. "What about the guest house you wanted to build down beside Swindlers Creek?"

Bill shook his head.

The last hour of the journey passed in silence. Evelyn was surprised when no one came outside to greet them as they pulled up at the Chalet.

"Where are Cecil and Nell and Len?"

"Oh, I forgot to tell you. They've gone to Mt Buffalo."

17
A Delicate Situation

Jean Goldsworthy gazed balefully out the window. It was snowing heavily.

"It's not letting up, Ross."

Her husband came over to the window and stood behind her. With his hands resting on her shoulders, his eyes followed hers.

They had been dreading this moment for several weeks. MacLelland, the manager of the Mt Buffalo Chalet, had been promising to send staff over to help them as soon as the weather improved. They had specific instructions not to turn to Bill Spargo for assistance. But the weather didn't improve. It got worse. Now the crisis was upon them. The ski season was in full swing.

The Goldsworthys, a newly married young couple, had left their home in Wandiligong, and the orchard they managed with Ross's father, as the successful applicants for the brand-new job of managing the Hotham Heights Chalet at Mt Hotham for the Victorian Railways. It looked like a good way to augment their income during these terrible Depression years. They had seen snow before on the distant mountain tops, but this was their first time meeting it up close - touching it, walking on it, living in it. Bill Spargo might have prioritised gold mining over chalet management, but Ross and Jean Goldsworthy had no experience of either.

*

"Look, Ross, there he is now!"

Bill Spargo was walking up the road - or rather, where the road had once been - towards them. He carried a pack on his back, as always. There were skis on his feet. Where he was heading, and why, was anyone's guess, but the weather had partially cleared, and it was a fine day for a walk. The wind, as always, was strong, but patches of blue poked through between the clouds.

"Let's grab him while we can!"

They had rung the head office of the Victorian Railways in Melbourne several days earlier in desperation. The instructions had been clear. They would have to find staff locally on the mountain. When Ross had explained that the only other people on the mountain were Bill Spargo and Evelyn Piper, they were advised to approach them. He felt sick about the idea.

"I doubt if he'll take on the job, after the way he's been treated."

"Well, ask him anyway. Offer him whatever he wants. Keep him happy. We can't afford to make a mess of this."

The Goldsworthys walked down through the deep snow to meet Bill. They had met each other a few times briefly, but that was all. Ross spoke first.

"Hello there, Bill. Nice day."

Bill nodded. Through his mind ran all the problems the Goldsworthys would be facing right now. He couldn't imagine how they would begin to cope, but that was not his problem. Besides, he had plenty of his own.

No point in beating around the bush, thought Ross to himself.

"Bill, would you and Evelyn come and work for us? We can't cope by ourselves, and you know this place backwards." Then he added as an afterthought, "I know you've had a rough time, but that was the Railways, not us."

Bill's mind was racing. It was the answer to their prayers. It was already a struggle out at the cabin. Evelyn was not happy at all. Still, he was angry at the way he had been treated. Why shouldn't the Railways stew in their own juice? This problem was entirely of their own making. Then again, to knock back an offer like this would be like cutting off his nose to spite his face, surely...

Ross was a little unnerved by Bill's silence.

"We'll look after you, Bill. The Railways are desperate right now. They'll offer you anything - anything that's reasonable. What do you think?"

Bill took a couple of steps forward, and offered his hand.

18
A Golden Year

It had been another long, busy, action-packed day - but then, what day wasn't like that up here in the snow? Ross and Jean lay side by side in the narrow bed. Normally, the skiers settled down well at night, but they were now a little rowdier than usual. It had been clear from the outset that Bill had run a loose ship, and there was an urgent need to instil a little discipline. These skiers had been allowed to develop some bad habits, too much late-night carousing being high on the list. They would probably settle down soon. Ross had introduced a strict 'lights out at midnight' policy, but he liked to be asleep well before then. Every day started early.

The partnership with Bill and Evelyn was working out better than they could have dreamed, though it had to be admitted they were an odd couple. Evelyn was so fastidious, cleaning the brown linoleum floors to a bright sheen with the old, discarded kerosene-soaked towels tied onto a broom handle. Bill, on the other hand, was very rough and ready. Earlier this evening they had caught him stashing dirty pots and pans away under the kitchen sink. The two of them got on well most of the time, but they had seen Evelyn fly at Bill occasionally.

"Ross, I think you'd better have a gentle word to our guests!"

The racket from the dining room was showing no signs of letting up, and it was getting late.

Ross sighed. The room cooled quickly once the fire began to die down, and he was reluctant to leave the warm bed.

"Yes, I guess I'll have to."

He was back soon.

"I think they'll be OK now. I read the riot act to them. A bit too much rum and raspberry on board."

There was nobody else they knew like Bill, that was for sure! They'd never met anybody so conscious of not wasting anything. Jean chuckled at the memory of seeing the cats making their way over to Kipper Villa the previous day.

"I can't believe he took that fish!"

Ross grunted in agreement. They had found a layer of blue mould covering a box of pickled kippers. They had wiped it off with an oily cloth, but the next day it was back, thicker than ever. The fish would have to go in the bin. But no! Bill had whisked them off to a nearby hut built by the cattlemen, the Lawlers, where he was living by himself. It was Lawler's Hut no more, however. It was 'Kipper Villa' now, and the cats could not resist it.

"Thank God they've finally shut up!"

Jean gave her young husband a soft kiss on the cheek, and rolled over to go to sleep.

*

It was certainly not ideal having a three-foot-deep channel of water running across a ski run. If you were designing the ideal run from scratch, it was the very last feature you would ever choose to include. Unfortunately, however, they had had no choice. It didn't really matter where you chose to ski at Mt Hotham, if you were starting from the top of the hill and heading down to Swindlers Creek, you were going to bump into the Brandy Creek water race - the famous 'Cobungra Ditch.' it started from near the headwaters of the creek and ran for about ten miles, following the contour of the hillside, falling ever so slightly as it went, carrying water for the hydraulic sluicing at the Brandy Creek Gold Mine that had impressed him so much.

It was a great place to take photos, though. Bill loved to position himself there with his camera. A bridge had been built, but it was very narrow, and many a skier had come to grief trying to navigate it at high speed. Photos of skiers travelling fast were spectacular, but more spectacular still were high speed crashes! Yes, it was cruel - some might even say sadistic - but the opportunity was just too good to pass up. Most of the skiers were not seriously hurt. Mind you, they had all held their breath when Warrand Begg, the President of the Melbourne University Ski Club, had taken a particularly nasty tumble. He had emerged covered with mud and blood but, amazingly, was none the worse for wear when they had had a chance to assess his injuries properly. The ditch had been 'Begg's Bath' ever since!

*

He had had a skinful. To be fair, it was probably only half a skinful, and he seemed to be a genial drunk. Evelyn was enjoying the conversation, and she would keep cracking walnuts for him for as long as he wanted to eat them.

"Why don't you stay on working for us?"

Bracher was making a tour of inspection of Mt Hotham on behalf of the Victorian Railways and it was clear that, after a very shaky start, operations were running very smoothly indeed. He had heard of the weekly trips that Ross and Bill made together to Mt St Bernard, six miles distant, to pick up the mail. He had heard of their trek down to Harrietville to pick up a large box of butter, carrying back half the box each on their shoulders. He had certainly heard of Evelyn's hard work around the Chalet, cooking and cleaning, and of her easy-going, friendly personality.

"You like working here, don't you?"

She agreed that she did.

"Well then, why don't you stay with us? You don't want to be chasing around the mountains with that old introvert. You'd be well looked after, you know."

It wasn't a very complimentary description of Bill, but she'd heard worse. Why was she so devoted to him? Why did she not jump at Bracher's offer? She did not doubt his sincerity. Bill was deep in financial trouble, that was clear to all. He didn't even bother to open most of his mail, but his debts were not hers, and anyway, it made not the slightest dent in his sense of independence and freedom. You can't get blood from a stone, after all. She admired his courage, his singlemindedness. She related strongly to his deep love of the mountains. It is true, he was not a warm man, not very expressive and not particularly affectionate, but he was honest, in his own way, and faithful. Would a bureaucrat like Bracher understand any of this? She smiled, cracked another walnut, and passed it over.

*

Bill saw the flash of lightning, and stood still, waiting for the thunder. He had counted to ten by the time it had arrived, and then it came as a low rumble, far beyond the horizon. Good! There was time to get back to the Chalet. That was the best place to be right now - not that anywhere would be entirely safe. His mind went back to that terrible storm several years earlier. It had come in the middle of summer. It would be difficult to convince most people that a summer storm could be far more dangerous than a winter blizzard, but it was true. The power of a lightning flash was extraordinary. It had punched a great hole in the thick stone external wall of the Chalet, and wreaked havoc inside. Cement and plaster had been torn from an inner wall, the panels of a wooden door had been splintered, and it had burnt all the rubber sheathing from the electric wires under the roof. All this in the blink of an eye. Bill had had to leave the mountain for a week after that, just to recover from the shock. He still felt he was lucky to be alive. His legs were feeling weak and shaky. His stomach was starting to churn. Yes, he would make it back to the Chalet, but he still would not be safe. There was no haven at Mt Hotham at the height of a thunderstorm.

*

It was time for the Goldsworthys to leave the mountain. They had been offered another year, but they had had enough. Besides, Ross's father was struggling with the orchard. The cosy valley of Wandiligong beckoned once more.

Note on the back of the photo (Evelyn's hand):
"On ramp at Hotham Heights
Ross and Jean and family and me 1933"

Evelyn standing with Ross and Jean Goldsworthy on the back verandah of their Wandiligong home.

19
A Brass Fortune?

There is more than one way to skin a cat. The discovery of a rich gold deposit would be wonderful, but poverty is poverty, wealth is wealth, and money is money. Bill had been sure he was onto a winner when he designed these brass keels for his skis! His wooden skis had been a real handful, especially on the steeper slopes. They shook all over the place when he was running in a straight line, and traversing a steep slope like this was an absolute nightmare! He couldn't get any grip, and had felt he was going to be thrown hundreds of feet down the mountain at any moment.

The shaded, icy section of the slope behind him, Bill paused as he emerged once again into the sunlight. The keels had been an absolute godsend. He had suddenly been able to ski with so much more speed and confidence. They worked much like the keel of a ship, stopping the skis from sliding sideways. He had had them specially made down in Melbourne.

There was a time there when he had been sure they would make him the fortune he so desperately wanted. He had planned to take out a patent on the design, but decided at the last minute to check with his friend Tom Mitchell before proceeding. Tom had learned to ski in Europe. He was wealthy and smart, and just about the best skier in Australia! Alas, Tom had broken the bad news to him. Steel edges on the skis did everything the brass keels did, and more. They were very popular in Europe. They hadn't come to Australia yet, but they soon would. The keels had no future at all. Tom was quite sure of that.

Bill had been bitterly disappointed at first to receive this news, but was also grateful to Tom for his honesty. He had potentially saved Bill a lot of money! No, there was no way around it. He was going to have to discover gold after all!

20
A Cold Night (November, 1933)

The mail car pulled to a halt. It was already dark, and the driver was keen to head back down the mountain. Evelyn was returning from a trip to Melbourne, and the plan had been for Bill to meet her on the road at Buckland's Cap, one and a half miles short of St Bernard Hospice. From there it was a six mile walk into Hotham. Fair enough, but where was Bill? She waited for a while, but it started to rain so

[I] shouldered my baggage case, parcel and bulging handbag and started to walk [as she wrote in her journal several months later]. *Getting darker, and case getting heavier. Presently kicked a piece of rope on the road so fixed case on my back. Kept going, wondering what could have happened to Will. The jaunty pioneering air fast failing. Not a sound but the tread of my shoes on the track. It was dark by then, no moon. I'd wandered 2 miles if I'd walked a yard, when out of the night stepped William, his relief boundless. Thought car had gone over the side. Driver had put me off at a gap, but one 6 miles from the Hospice. Night became like ink, rain pouring off face and neck. We walked on a mile, feeling for the road like the blind feeling for the curb. An incautious step and over the side into space. Will somehow located the Hospice's "cubby house" exactly half a corrugated water tank used for store dump in winter when snow prevents cars getting further. W[illiam]. was sure if we kept going, we should go over and end the heartache... So we crawled in like rabbits in a hutch. Wet and shivering and too cramped and cold to sleep.*

Crawled out like foxes at 4 a. m. No wonder it was cold. Everywhere white with snow (and beautiful to behold) my feet and hands so cold could have cried with it. (I didn't!) but groaned as I straightened out

aching stiff limbs. Warmed up as we walked to Hospice 6 o'clock and all abed. Lit the fire and thawed out, breakfast, and 6 miles tramp to Hotham. Cheery, warm welcome and early lunch with Mr and Mrs G[oldsworthy].

21
A Change of Plan

Bill was shocked to arrive at the adit one morning and find nobody there. He had expected the two miners to be hard at work. They had been grumbling about their wages for a while, but that was nothing new. It had never been easy finding the money to pay them, but it had been a lot harder after his lease at the Chalet had been cancelled. What was he to do? He would have given them more money if he had had it. He made his way down to their camp. Nothing there but flattened grass and a cold fire. Looked like they were serious this time.

They'd given it a red-hot go. They'd driven tunnels on both sides of Swindlers Valley. They'd found small amounts of gold, but not a lot. Certainly nothing like the deep lead at Brandy Creek. Maybe the northern continuation he had dreamed of all these years simply didn't exist. Maybe the symmetry of those two saddles, and the way they lined up so neatly, was nothing more than coincidence. Who could say? Ah well, looked like it was time for a change of plan.

22
An Angry, Frustrated Woman

(Excerpts from Evelyn's journal, February - March 1934)

Monday, 5th February

W[illiam] S[pargo] came over with an axe to sharpen. As usual brought parcel of rations little things - mint, parsley, 2 or 3 new potatoes and such things to supplement our menus which sadly lack fresh food. I was bread baking but not old or wise enough at the job to carry on in face of interruptions - consequently looked in vain for the next two hours for any sign of my dough rising.

Tuesday, 6th February

Dough and me both sad as putty! Got to brew a fresh lot of yeast and start at the whole job over again.

Thursday, 8th February

107 degrees of heat in Melbourne

Friday, 9th February

The heat up at this altitude worse than before. No good to health at all. And the flies a plague to drive one crazy, wild and lurid.

Saturday, 10th February

Temperature in Melbourne highest recorded

Monday, 19th February

Oh God how utterly weary I am of all of it. To stay here if one loved would be bad enough - always alone, never seeing anything but dead gaunt trees, a dreary dull companion, never whistles a tune, never a joke, living on yourself. Your mind growing inwards alone with your aching yearning heart.

Tuesday, 20th February

Desperate with the whole rotten show. The muddling, the setbacks - most of it through lack of 'guts' and a man who has no more courage or assurance than a caterpillar. If the mountain was gold right through I wouldn't be fettered here soul and spirit another hour. Dear God its awful to live forever in grappling irons, spirit in revolt to want to do that which every fibre of my being says do, "Get Out" and another whispering, "Stick it out for Steve's sake."

Carrying the whole thru on my shoulders. If we ever win through it will be because I spurred (not inspired - some men you can't inspire) him to do things and carry things through.

It's a man's job really.

Wednesday, 28th February

<u>Across the Table</u>

We sit across the table, you and I, who might have loved so well,
and talk, and fill our glasses up with wine,
and I wear white,
Because I heard you say, once long ago,
"In white with flowers at her breast",
But I have taken away the pale flowers
Lest you should bury there your head
And weep among them.
And that would spoil the pretty comedy
we act so well.

Monday, 5th March

Dad sent me Pickwick and Nicholas Nickleby. I remember long, long ago a girl not yet 14½ years old. Little maid-of-all-work. Lonely young soul of Mrs Hunt's Young Ladies School and Kindergarten. Her room a rambling old attic away from all human warmth and friendship. At night, a burning candle stuck with candle-wax to the seat of the room's solitary chair. The flickering light throwing eerie shadows in the dark nooks and crannies of the dismal old attic. In bed to keep warm, the little lonely girl pouring over a book, trembling fearfully for poor Nicholas and his fine, brave friendship for poor wretched Smike.

Thursday, 8th March

Mrs Pridham writes that Steve is well and "behaving quite well and is a very good tempered and well-meaning boy."

Saturday, 10th March

Went to Hotham and stayed night. Halo Hats all the rage. Never wore a bowler, now shall miss wearing a halo.

Hope [St] Peter will make a note of it and remember when the time comes that its "just my luck" and I never had a chance... and let me don one on probation up alone.

Sunday, 11th March

Half the trouble in life is caused, not by what people think of us, but what we think they are thinking of us.

Thursday, 15th March

Received Application Payment form from Repatriation requiring signature. Great hopes that M[embers] of P[arliament] have renewed Allow[ance] after all. No one up here qualified to sign.

Almost making a journey of 50 miles into Omeo to have paper witnessed but instead expended much time and thought in wording a letter to Shire Secretary Omeo. Polite refusal for my pains, and in meantime notified that form sent in error!!

Sunday, 18th March

Mrs Goldsworthy arrived unexpectedly to see "Dutch Hut" and say farewell.

Thursday, 22nd March

Mr and Mrs G[oldsworthy] left Hotham today.

Saturday, 24th March

It is very cold and the fire as usual a smoking brute when the wind blows strong and bleakly. All day pouring over food catalogues and price lists ordering supplies for the winter. Soon shall be snowed in again I suppose.

23
The Elegy

It had been a frustrating day, rummaging through old newspapers for the spelling of a single word. She had recently written an 'elegy' to the Goldsworthys, a celebration of their year together. Memories had flooded her mind. There had been that spectacular crash when she and Jean had collided on their skis and fallen heavily on the hard icy ground in a tangled heap. She would have cried with pain if she hadn't been laughing so much! Then there were the skiers - a great bunch of educated, refined, people. It was such a thrill to be in their company! Two stood out particularly - Fanny Strauss, the gentle, kind, fun-loving Secretary of the Melbourne University Ski Club, and the club's austere President. Then there was the little dog, Brenda, who had come to them in such poor condition, nearly dead from distemper. She had rallied on a diet of eggs, and filings from a copper penny. The landscape and the weather were a huge part of the experience, too, especially the early morning 'mystic seas', when dense cloud filled the valleys, leaving the highest peaks and ridges to stand out above it like islands and promontories. She had begun to write.

Requiem for the Late Host and Hostess of Hotham whose experience, and consequent enforced isolation in "Snow-man's land", as Manager and Manageress of Hotham Heights, must surely be a unique beginning to married bliss - an experiment which few just starting life together care to put to the test in these restless, pleasure loving days.

Elegy Written Upon the Mountains

*It really won't be quite the same, old Hotham
Without the worthy Goldies in command.
To ski ten miles across the snow was worth it
To meet that combination of a smile.*

*But now the bleak hills' bleakest phase is nothing
To the cold that in my heart has come to stay.
It feels as if the sun had fled the mountains,
That light has gone from even the sunniest day.*

*The skiing folk will miss the little hostess,
Who beamed on them her sunny-natured smile;
The host who held the magic key to promptness,
To porridge hot instead of merely mild.*

*Herr Strauss will Begg in vain for treble helpings.
His porridge bowl will be the normal size.
No more will youthful matron rule the kitchen
With softened heart, and tactfulness, so wise.*

*There was never any fuss or consternation,
Not even when a score and ten were there.
Peace reigned, even among the motley,
When food was "on the air".*

And in the kitchen, piled about her dishes,
Three foot high on table, and on chair,
Even Brenda underneath the table
Maintained the savoir fair.

When the temperature was nigh approaching zero,
And demand on buttered toast was super high,
The heroes never failed to pack a relay
To replenish the supply.

Even would I suffer semi-annihilation
Upon the slope that runs from Hotham house
If on the ski we might career together,
And repeat that comic posture on the ice.

And now between the apple blo' and nut trees
Tony and Jean will go their happy way,
Dreaming in leisure moments in old Wandy
Of sunsets, mystic seas, and those early days.

But an irritating little thorn lay deep in the heart of it all. Was 'Herr' spelt with one 'r' or two? There was nobody up here she could ask. Bill didn't know, and she could hardly ask the Goldsworthys. She might with some considerable difficulty (and a bit of luck!) bail up a cattleman, but what were the chances that any of them would know? No, she was going to have to solve this little problem herself, and the only way she could think of to do that was to start poring through old newspapers. Eventually she found it. There were two 'r's in 'Herr', but it had taken her all day to be sure!

She wrote the poem out one final time, in green ink, and placed it between two thick sheets of brown cardboard. She punched two holes through the cardboard and the poem, and tied it all together with a matching green ribbon. Then she placed it in an envelope, and put it in the post.

*

Jean was hanging out the washing when she heard the postman's whistle. There was a mystery parcel amongst the handful of letters when she walked down to the mailbox shortly after. She turned it over in her hands. Sender: E. Piper, Hotham Heights. What could Evelyn possibly be sending her? It was barely a week since they had last spoken to each other.

She took it inside and opened it carefully. As she began to read, tears filled her eyes.

"Ross! Come here, quickly! Look at this!"

As Ross began to read Evelyn's poem he placed his arm around his wife's shoulders. They finished it together, and embraced at the end.

Jean and Ross would treasure Evelyn's 'Elegy' for the rest of their lives.

Note on the back of the photo (Bill's hand):
"Mt Loch and Mt Feathertop above the clouds Aust Alps"
These are the "mystic seas" referred to in the final line of Evelyn's "Elegy."

24
Life at the Cabin

Evelyn heard it first - a high-pitched cry. At first she dismissed it as coming from a bird, but it was insistent, and sounded very much like a human. A woman - maybe even a girl. But how could that be? A lost skier, perhaps, but nobody would ever approach from that direction. Only Bill and she were crazy enough to climb up to Bill's cabin from Swindlers Creek. It was a steep climb, there was no track, and the snow was deep. Besides, what would be the point?

She stepped out of the cabin and moved around to the southern end, just in time to see a figure emerge from the trees and stagger onto the small plateau.

"Help! Help!" The cry was unmistakable now.

She ran back to the front door. "Bill! Bill! Quickly! There's somebody in trouble!" She retraced her footsteps, and made her way towards the source of the cries. Whoever she was, she was not wearing skis or snowshoes. The snow rose well above her knees. Evelyn was herself not dressed for the snow, she had run outside in such a hurry, and found herself also floundering. Bill arrived at her side just as she reached the poor girl. Standing on either side of her, each with one of her arms draped across their shoulders, Bill and Evelyn staggered back to the cabin.

The story came out in fits and bursts. Bill and Evelyn encouraged her to calm down and recover first. The poor girl was sobbing, but clearly felt a sense of urgency, and had an important message to give. She was Beryl Williams, the niece of the Gribbles, who had taken over the management of Hotham Heights following the departure of the Goldsworthys. The boiler at the Chalet - responsible for all the hot water - had recently frozen and cracked during an early bout of frost. The Chalet now had no hot water, and a large number of skiers were expected in a few days for the King's Birthday long weekend.

A party of experienced skiers was bringing a replacement boiler in over the snow-covered plains from Cobungra. Beryl's uncle had planned to take them provisions, but had injured his knee while skiing. He had fired a gun on numerous occasions to try to attract Bill's attention. (Bill and Evelyn had heard nothing.) As a last resort this plucky seventeen-year-old had offered to deliver the message herself. She had left the Chalet at 11.30 am. It was now past four. For much of the journey, the snow had been waist deep. It was a miracle she had reached them at all!

Bill left immediately. Evelyn changed Beryl into dry clothes, put her to bed, and gave her a steaming mug of tea.

Bill walked through the night, catching up with the party shortly after dawn. The boiler was on a horse-drawn buggy, but eventually the snow became too deep for the horses. It was then transferred to a sledge, and dragged in by the men themselves. It took them two days.

Eventually a party of skiers arrived at the cabin to take Beryl back to the Chalet.

The epic journey of Beryl Williams was reported in The Argus newspaper in Melbourne. Evelyn Piper was described as Bill's cousin.

*

She sat comfortably on a large, rounded lump of granite. The wind tore at her clothing and the mist swirled around her, but she clutched determinedly at the pad and pencil she held in her hands. Evelyn loved to write. There was something about the process of putting pen to paper, of creating something where before there had been nothing, that stirred her imagination. Language. Words. Sentences. And poetry. Of course, there was no way she could make a living from it, but it certainly helped to make the poverty a little more bearable. The mere act of writing lifted her spirits so much, it was an end in itself. She always felt better after writing a little verse to send to Steven, and hopefully he appreciated them, too. Could writing ever mean more to her than this? Could she dare to dream?

*

Evelyn put down the latest letter from her father - her most adored, and adoring father, back in England - and sighed. He would love it up here...the snow, the deep sense of serenity, the pureness of it all. They had both fantasised about winning the lottery, or striking it rich in some other way, and having the time and means to properly enjoy life, and each other's company. She could be open and honest with her father in a way that she couldn't with Bill. He was under so much pressure himself. Her father was worried about her, though. Her life sounded so hard. There wasn't much he could do from such a great distance, but his letters were a great comfort, nonetheless. As a gesture of his deep and abiding affection for her, he had even written out Keats' poem, 'Endymion', in full: "A thing of beauty is a joy forever..." Good old Dad. He was a rock!

*

It was a tough life that Bill had chosen for himself, no question about that. It was too late to turn back now, though - death or glory. He lifted the rusty old sheet of corrugated iron that he had been carrying on his back off the grass, and slung it across the low branches of a nearby snow gum. Then he stood back to have a good look at it. It didn't appear very stable. There was every chance it would fall during the night and land on him. He placed one end on the ground, leaving the other end up in the tree. That looked better. It didn't matter all that much, really. He doubted it would rain tonight, and the wind had dropped considerably.

Time to turn his attention to dinner. He threw some oats and water in the billy, and placed it over a little fire. He made sure to boil a little more than he needed. He would fry up the leftovers with a little bacon fat for breakfast tomorrow morning. He hadn't seen Evelyn or the cabin for a couple of days. Lucky she was so good at entertaining herself. He was over on the Diamantina Fall now, so named because any rain that landed here fell into the Diamantina River. He was well north of Swindlers Valley, and would lose too much time traipsing back and forth to the cabin every day. He was looking for reefs - quartz reefs near the surface that might contain gold. The 'deep lead dream' was dead. A pick and a shovel were the main tools of the trade. He was getting a little money from the government. The miners' susso had kept a lot of prospectors alive during these Depression years, but it wasn't much, and he felt guilty about taking it anyway. Maybe one day he'd be able to pay it back. He was grateful that Evelyn made so few demands on him. She had her reading and her writing, and loved just going for a wander. She knew this country nearly as well as he did now.

*

Alma Coleman was worried. She, her husband, Charles, and four other skiers were making their weary way up Swindlers Spur towards Mt Loch. They had been out ski touring on the Bogong High Plains for a week. The weather had been wonderful, but now, just as they were almost in sight of home, it was turning nasty. The fog was beginning to close in, and snow was falling heavily. They would need to keep close to the pole line. The group's morale was low, and dropping with every step.

Suddenly two figures emerged from the fog in front of them. Who were they? They appeared to have packs on their backs. As they came closer, it became clear. It was Bill Spargo, and his housekeeper, Evelyn Piper...and they were bearing hot coffee and scones. How did they know where and when to intercept their party? Their timing had been perfect! Alma would ponder these questions for the rest of her life, but the answers were never forthcoming.

*

Evelyn lay in the empty bed at the cabin, preparing to go to sleep. What a strange relationship they had! Mind you, she wasn't really complaining. The last thing she needed right now was to fall pregnant. Still, a man and a woman alone together in an isolated hut for months on end, it would be hardly surprising if...but Bill was not that kind of man. The occasional hug was about as far as it went. She could count on the fingers of one hand the number of times he had kissed her, and even then it had always been on the cheek!

*

Bill's eyes nearly popped out of his head as the plate of food was placed in front of him. Thick slices of roast beef covered with rich gravy, potatoes, pumpkin, peas... How long since he had eaten a meal like this? When Bill had first suggested he talk to Martin Romuld about getting a job with the State Electricity Commission at Pretty Valley, Evelyn had leapt at the idea. Their situation was desperate. She knew Bill and Martin went back a long way. Martin had trained in engineering in his native Norway, but had found work scarce, and come out to Australia. After a series of various jobs, he had been given a lead role in the development of the Kiewa Hydroelectric Scheme, based at the SEC Cottage on the Bogong High Plains. Martin was also a champion skier, and had stayed as a guest at the Chalet back in the days when Bill had been manager. Martin didn't owe Bill any favours, but Evelyn felt it was definitely worth a try.

Bill tucked into the food with eager anticipation - not just of the food, but of a well-paid position with the Commission. Over the course of the meal, however, his spirits slowly fell. Of course, he agreed, he was too old to work on the drills. Yes, he agreed, he didn't have the skills or training to be a carpenter. He could work as the cook's assistant. It wouldn't be much of a job - mostly chopping wood for the stoves - and the pay would not be much, either, but no doubt something better would turn up down the track. Bill nodded glumly. By the time the meal was finished, he had rejected the offer. Martin understood entirely. There were no hard feelings. At least he had had a good feed.

*

The Chalet was once again under new management. The Bradshaws seemed like nice people. When Bill was offered a job working there during the winter months, he agreed to do so.

Bill building the first chimney at the hut.

Evelyn wringing out clothes at the hut.

Life at the Cabin

Note on the back of the card (Evelyn's hand): "Nature forms this old Snow Man. It looks as though he is breathing the cold air (but this was just a mark on the negative) x"

Note on the back of the card (Evelyn's hand): "See the herring-bone tracks of the skis. That is how one climbs back after a lovely run. This is a famous ski course (lower end) of Hotham called the "Varsity Drag." It drops over 1,000 ft in a mile and they race it in 1 min. 38 sec. (but not Mum) x"

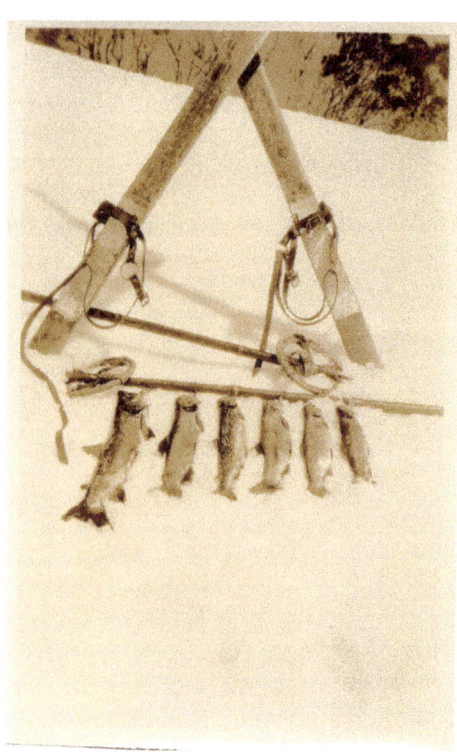

I strongly suspect this is one of Evelyn's compositions.

I wonder where this photo of Evelyn having a dip was taken. It looks too wide to be Swindlers Creek.

Note on the back of the photo: (Evelyn's hand) "Crossing the creek with the mails aboard for Hotham. Melting snow above."

"Forking the channel" (Evelyn's hand) Evelyn working on the channel that diverted water from the spring to the hut.

I don't know where this photograph of Evelyn cooking was taken, but she looks like she is enjoying herself!

Spargo's Hut in deep snow. We don't get snowfalls like this anymore!

Evelyn enjoying the view...

The structure beside the chimney is probably a damper to stop wind blowing down the chimney.

Evelyn peeping out above the deep banks of snow.

Life at the Cabin

Evelyn in snowshoes beside the hut.

I wonder if the structure on the left is a drying rack.

"At Hotham 1937" (Bill's hand) I expect Evelyn took this photo of Bill.

25
An Apartment in Melbourne

Evelyn placed her bag of groceries on the ground beside her, and reached into her coat pocket for the front door key. It was so good to be away from the mountains, away from the silence and the solitude, surrounded by noise and lights and people - so many people! Most importantly of all, it was so good to be away from Bill!

It had taken a while to sort out this compromise, but she knew she couldn't stay up there forever. She would have gone mad, alone in that tiny hut with him. Thank God she had her dressmaking skills! She had picked up enough work to cover food and rent, with a bit of money thrown in by her dear father every now and then. The budgeting was tight, but so far she was managing.

It was lovely to still return to the mountains periodically. She loved them as much as ever, but the living conditions were so harsh, and the future looked so bleak. Bill appreciated her more now, too. He didn't take her as much for granted, and made a real fuss over her when she arrived. That was nice.

Door open, she picked up the groceries, and walked into her tiny kitchen. She dumped the bag down upon a bench, put the kettle on, kicked off her shoes and collapsed into a chair. The city was everything that the mountains were not - ugly, loud and dirty. Right now, though, that was just fine with her!

26
Bella

Bill made himself comfortable on the bed beside the stove, and pulled out the latest of his mother's letters from the pocket of his coat. Bella wrote often - loving letters addressed to both Bill and Evelyn - and they were a great comfort, but it had been a while since the last one. She was plagued with mental health difficulties, and often apologised for not writing more frequently. She had episodes where she was as high as a kite, when she would not stop talking, could not sleep, did not eat, and became very thin. Then she would crash into a deep depression, and not leave the house for days. She felt guilty for being a burden on her daughters, Polly and Elsie, when she should have been helping them get on with their lives.

Bella had moved in with Polly the previous year, and they had recently decided to move house. The new place was much better than where they had been. They had been surrounded by noisy factories, and been plagued by flies from the stables behind them. It had also been very damp. The new house, still in Brunswick, was much more comfortable. It had a nice washhouse, and a bath with a chip heater. The rent was higher, but they were letting out one room to a boarder.

Polly had been working as live-in cook for a wealthy widow, Mrs Duckett, in the leafy suburb of Hawthorn. Large gardens surrounded the house, and swept right down to the Yarra River. Mrs Duckett had recently died following a brief illness. Polly had been kept extremely busy in the days leading up to her death, cooking for the three live-in nurses as well as Mrs Duckett. She had worn herself into the ground, and could barely talk by the end of it all. She had gone to the country for a couple of weeks to recover. Bella had been hoping that Polly might receive a small portion of the inheritance, but it was all being left to her two sons. She felt angry with Polly for exhausting herself pointlessly. The property would eventually be sold, but in the meantime the police were checking the house every night to make sure there were no break-ins. All the jewellery was kept in a safe. They had sacked the gardener and sold the cow, so she and Polly were no longer getting any cream. The garden was going downhill quickly. Bella was sure that Polly would never get another job as good as that again.

She apologised for not having replied to Bill's letters. She planned to send some newspapers up to him. Bill had turned fifty one week earlier, and she was keen to assure him she had not forgotten his birthday. She would clean his suit, and send it up to him with his dressing gown. The suit had been alive with silverfish at the other house, but she had managed to keep it clear of both silverfish and moths since then. She told Bill to tell Evelyn she would send up a copy of the Women's Weekly for her, and asked after Steven.

The following week, she was planning to send Bill a birthday cake - better late than never. She had ordered it the previous Thursday. It was the first time in a long time she had managed to get out of the house. She would send the cake in a wooden box, because a cardboard box would be too frail.

She was pleased that Bill was once again working at the Chalet. She worried about him being out at the cabin during the winter. She was heading out now to pick up the cake.

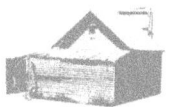

27
The End of the Road

Evelyn tossed her book aside. How had this life in the mountains, this exotic adventure in the wilds on the other side of the world, become so dull and tedious? Surely even life in England would be better than this! In the summer months, she barely saw Bill. He was off somewhere on some remote mountainside, digging his holes, eating his porridge from that revolting old billy caked on the inside with the porridge of years that he refused to clean, his cheese and potatoes, and catching his fish. Then in the winter he would spend most of the time in bed, only getting up occasionally to throw some more wood in the stove. He would happily spend hours sewing name tags into his underwear. Who was going to steal his undies, for Heaven's sake? Bill appeared to have an infinite capacity for boredom. And how many spoonsful of sugar can you add to a cup of cocoa, anyway?

The apartment in Melbourne had taken some of the pressure off but the truth was, they were going nowhere. They could die up here, and nobody would know for weeks. She had helped Bill with his mining activities when he could no longer afford to pay for labour. She had done some work over at the Feathertop Bungalow. It had all been fun for a while, but none of it was sustainable, none of it offered any prospect of a secure future. She was disappointed that Bill had refused Martin's offer to work for the Commission. Yes, it would have been a lowly position. Yes, it would not have been very well paid. Yes, it was a blow to his pride - a big one. She understood all that. But it would have been regular, year-round work, and a better offer may well have come up eventually. It might have just been enough. Then again, of course, it might not, too. Yes, he had picked up some winter work at the Chalet. It would pay better than her work at the Bungalow and would help a little, but not a lot. There was no light at the end of the tunnel. What was she to do?

Bill, at least, put no pressure on her to stay. He appeared to understand the hopelessness of her position, and she appreciated that.

*Note on the back of the photo (Bill's hand):
"Starting of the first tunnel, Nov 1933,
on the Vic Alps"*

28
Mother and Son Reunited

Evelyn was excited. She would be back in Britain for Christmas. She hesitated to use the word 'home'. Where exactly was her home now? How old would Steven be? Sixteen! He was only ten when she had seen him last. He must have changed so much! It would have been tough for him, going through his teenage years with his grandparents. How much would they remember of their lives at his age? Still, they were kind people. She was sure they would have looked after him well and, of course, much of that time he had spent in boarding school. Yes, they had been in constant touch through letters, but that was no substitute for face to face contact.

There was talk of war brewing in Europe. Who knew what this would mean? Would Steven have to fight? Might her own life even be at risk? No doubt she would have been safer back in Australia, but a mother's place is by her son in times of danger.

Would she ever see Bill again? Did she even want to see Bill again? Yes, she decided, she did, but their relationship had changed a great deal over the years. Still, all relationships changed with time, surely. Initial excitement gave way to familiarity, but with it, hopefully, came a rich contentment and intimacy. It was strange how they had lived for all those years so close to each other without any sexual relationship. No doubt if she told most people, they would not believe her. Still, the proof was in the pudding, and the fact was that there was no pudding, no 'bun in the oven'. Just as well. Bill had never expressed any interest in parenthood, and had no income to support a family, anyway.

What was Bill's future? His search for gold had never faltered in its intensity, despite his lack of success. Did he really care if he found gold or not? Was the search sufficient in itself? He certainly loved the lifestyle, but she couldn't imagine any other man on Earth putting up with conditions like that. It was so hard! Well, she would have faith in him for as long as he had faith in himself. It was all he lived for. Knowing Bill, she would not be at all surprised if he turned up trumps one day. If anyone could succeed under conditions like these, it was him. She leaned over the rail, peeling her eyes for the sight of an albatross, but all that lay ahead of her was an empty sky, and a slate grey ocean.

29
Bill All Alone

Pearl Bradshaw stood and watched with wonder as Bill Spargo strode down the road away from her. It was a sight she had seen many times before, but it still filled her with wonder. With a great, heavy pack on his back, no doubt filled mostly with potatoes - perhaps also some flour and cheese - he would follow the road as far as the top of the Varsity Drag. Then he would plunge down the ski run, now covered with rocks, low bushes and grass, to Swindlers Creek. He would follow the creek downstream for a period, then he would cross it, and climb up the steep hillside opposite to the tiny plateau where his little cabin stood. Nobody would be there to greet him. He would light his stove and make himself comfortable. It might be weeks before he made the journey out again. How did he put up with the loneliness?

She and Jim were enjoying their time as managers of the Hotham Heights Chalet. They had taken over from the Gribbles in time for the 1937 ski season. Bill didn't appear to have worked much for the Gribbles, but Jim and Pearl were very glad to have him on board. He was such a good worker. He appeared to be able to rise to any challenge. No job was too heavy or too dirty, and he seldom asked for assistance. He certainly never complained about anything. Ever.

What a strange bird he was, though. So sensitive, and so easily embarrassed. Something of a romantic, too. She remembered the time he had gathered some wildflowers for her, and turned as red as a beetroot when one of the young housemaids had cheekily asked if the flowers were for her! She was always 'Mrs Bradshaw' to him - never Pearl. Then there was the time he had sat down to join them at the dinner table, and had given the Worcestershire sauce bottle a good shake, not realising the lid was off. Sauce had flown everywhere, and poor Bill had nearly died of embarrassment! He was quite pompous in his own way, too. He refused to eat tomato sauce. That was an insult to the cook, he said. And no sense of humour. She had joked once that if their nine-month-old son, Peter, did not sprout some teeth soon, she would have to get him some false ones. Bill had reacted with alarm. He had taken her seriously!

Poor old fellow. He loved a good meal of roast beef. They would always give him the leftovers if there were any. He certainly couldn't afford to buy it himself. He tried to grow his own vegetables, but the cold made it difficult. He had even been experimenting with the local plants, working out which ones were edible, and which were not.

It was hypnotic watching his easy, regular gait. She shook herself out of her reverie as he passed the corner and disappeared.

30
Fire!

It had been a frightening afternoon. Pearl had been out riding with her father and a young housemaid. Suddenly, at about four o'clock, the sky had turned dark as night. The riders were disoriented, but fortunately, the horses knew the way home. They had yarded the horses, but left the sliprails down in case they had wanted to leave in the event of fire. They were confident the Chalet would not burn. Nevertheless, they had made preparations, filling the bath with water, and wetting some blankets.

At about six thirty, just as they were sitting down to dinner, a roar came up the valley from out of the Dargo. Pearl and Jim looked at each other in alarm. Jim sprinted up into the attic.

The phone rang. Pearl answered it.

"This is the Omeo exchange. Are you all OK up there?"

"Yes, thanks, we're fine."

Jim came racing down from the attic.

"The attic's on fire!"

Pearl quickly changed her tune.

"Looks like we've got to go! Jim says the house is on fire. We've got to leave!

She banged down the receiver.

Jim made the snap decision that their best chance lay with a small shed above a well that had been built many years before by Bill. He held up some barbed wire fencing for Pearl to climb through. Pearl was carrying Peter, their infant son.

"I can't, Jim! I can't get through there!"

"Well, you'll have to jump the sliprails, then."

They were down on the ground at one end. Pearl leaped over, and they dashed to the well. The shed had a little door, with a small glass window. Like the double-glazed windows of the Chalet, it had been shattered by the heat. Pearl and the housemaid settled into a routine. They would dip a blanket into the well, then hold it up in the space where the window had been. It would be bone dry in seconds. They would then repeat the process.

It was a long night. Pearl pondered. How had they been caught so unawares? It had been a hot, dry summer. Fires had been racing across the state for weeks. They had been reported to the east, over on the Bogong High Plains, and she and Jim had been climbing nearby Mt Higginbotham for the last few nights, checking on their progress. The red blazes stood out clearly against the black sky. They appeared to have passed them by. But the fire that caught them had come up from the west.

At dawn they gingerly stepped outside. The fire had gone, but it had left devastation in its wake. All that remained of the Chalet were the original stone walls and the chimney. The roof and all the wooden extensions, including the ramp from the attic, were gone. They picked their way through the ruins, assessing the damage, trying to find something that had escaped the heat. They had lost everything - money, jewellery, clothes, possessions.

Pearl found a small tin. It was blackened, but the shape suggested it contained Camp Pie. She was hungry.

"Look, Jim! This might be OK!"

But when she shook it, it rattled. Picking through the debris she found several more, but none of them contained anything edible.

"No, it's no good. They're all the same."

Jim wiped his hand across his brow, and surveyed the scene around him.

"You know, we need to start thinking about where we're going to spend the night. It must be about midday already. I was hoping some help would have arrived by now, but maybe it's not going to come at all."

Pearl frowned in thought. "You're right, Jim. They might not even know we're in trouble."

The bedraggled little party walked down to the road and began the long march to Harrietville, 19 miles away. They had only been walking about an hour, however, when they heard the sound of a truck changing gears. It was Vic Wraith, from the general store! Once on board, they heard his story. The woman on the phone from the Omeo exchange had relayed their message of distress. Vic and his partner had left Harrietville at dawn, but it had taken them seven hours to get this far, removing all the dead cattle and burnt trees from the road.

Passing Mt St Bernard, they picked up Barney Rush and his family and staff. The Hospice had also burnt down. They had found safety by the bank of a nearby creek.

Pearl and Jim also came across their dairy cow, Carey, and her calf, quite unscathed.

The Bradshaws would eventually return to Mt Hotham, but Carey would not. From then on, it would be powdered milk only for the skiers.

The burnt out remains of the Hotham Heights Chalet after the 1939 fire. One whole wing of the stone building has disappeared, leaving only the massive chimney.

31
Meanwhile, over at Golden Point...

The sky turned dark in the middle of the afternoon for Bill, just as it had for Pearl. It was time to abandon the day's work and return to his cabin. He could see fire in the distance. Should he try to get off the mountain altogether? But no. It was too late for that. The fire was already charging up Swindlers Valley towards him. Suddenly, another line of fire sprang up between him and his cabin. It threatened to cut him off.

He realised there was only one thing he could do. It was a desperate move, but this was a desperate moment. Moving around to the side of the fire front, he noted that the line had small gaps in a few places. Running as fast as he could, he made for one of these. He could barely see, and his throat and chest filled with smoke. The flames were so close he could have reached out and touched them.

Then he was through the worst of it, and walking on black ashes. The deathly quiet was eerie. There were no bird calls, nor any signs of life. As he approached the cabin, however, he came across bush which had not yet been burnt. This was an encouraging sign. It may yet be standing!

What a wonderful sight it was, as he broke free from the forest of snow gum and walked out onto the little plateau, to see his sturdy little cabin just as he had left it, waiting for his return! Now he was home, and able to fight the fire on his own terms. But there was no time to lose. It would be upon him soon, no question about that.

Bill had long ago planned for this. This was partly the reason why he had chosen to build so close to a spring. Indeed, with Evelyn's assistance, he had diverted part of it so that it ran right to his hut. He carried his large, galvanised iron bath into the hut, and filled it with water. Next, he filled every small vessel he could find - every pot, every billycan, every cup or mug. Lastly, he saturated his clothes with water. He then entered the hut, closed the door, placed a wet towel over his mouth, and waited.

He didn't have to wait long. Suddenly, it was upon him with a roar. Parts of the interior woodwork began to burst into flame, but he was able to douse the flames with water. The heat and smoke were so intense, he was tempted to run outside. Only the knowledge that it was even worse out there held him back. Drops of boiling oil began to splatter onto the top of his head. The waterproof malthoid that lined the under-surface of the ceiling was melting! He grabbed a kerosene box, and threw it over his head.

At times he lay on the floor, gasping for breath, trying to get below the smoke, but he could never stay there for long. New flames kept springing up. It was touch and go for a long while, but at last the inferno subsided, and he was able to go outside and put out the last of the fires. He had loaded his shotgun, to be used as a last resort to prevent death by incineration, but it stood where he had placed it, untouched. He had been almost blinded by smoke, and could barely speak for the next two days.

*

The fires had torn through the mountains - and most of Victoria's forested areas - on Friday 13th January 1939, 'Black Friday.' On Tuesday 17th January, The Age reported that "Mr W. B. Spargo of Mt. Hotham" was missing. On Wednesday 8th February, nearly three weeks later, the Wangaratta Chronicle Despatch carried an account of Mr Spargo's successful battle against the fires. The Herald carried a report from Bill to readers in Melbourne the following day.

Lonely Heights

A note comes through today from Victoria's most elevated resident – Mr. Spargo of Hotham Heights. At the moment he may also be the loneliest citizen in the State.

"I don't want to say anything about the great fire," he writes: "no more than that all Hell let loose here. I want to forget all about it. It has been rather depressing here, with the country looking more like Arabia than the Australian Alps, and with everything knocked out of plumb. Transport and telephone went phut. There are no neighbours left, and I am the only resident now on the mountain. It's all gone right back to scratch. Haven't had a paper since before the fire."

Let's hope that, after a good winter mantling of snow, Hotham will emerge with softer contours to its silent vistas.

*

On 3rd September 1939 the Prime Minister, Sir Robert Menzies, announced that Australia was at war.

32
Gold!

Evelyn sat down with a cup of tea and made herself comfortable before opening Bill's latest letter. Gosh, he sounded flat. It was understandable, though. He had worked so hard for so long, and suffered so much, and had so little to show for it all. Despite all his meticulous, methodical work, his circumstances had gradually deteriorated, not improved. Now he was alone - traumatised by the fires, too, no doubt. Yes, it was most definitely understandable. Yet in her heart, she felt sure this was the worst time to abandon his dream. No doubt he was feeling her absence keenly, but the Bradshaws would be back once the new Chalet had been built, and the mountain would start to fill up with people again. Bill's luck could turn at any time. Besides, if he did give up, where would he go? What would he do? How would he find meaning in his life?

Evelyn placed a pad of paper on the table before her, and picked up a pen to write a reply. She was touched faintly by guilt. It wasn't just Bill's dream. She had shared it with him for so long, it had become her dream as well. She was only starting to realise that now. If Bill abandoned his dream, he would be abandoning her dream too. Any faint hope she still harboured of one day living in luxury (or at least comfort) would be finally dashed to pieces. Yes, she knew, it was highly unlikely, but it was such a tantalising fantasy, and it had carried her so far for so long, she didn't want to let it go now. The words wrote themselves as the pen moved across the page: Don't give up now, Bill. You've come too far to let it go. I still believe in you, Bill. Keep going!

*

Evelyn woke up with a start. Where was she? What time was it? It was pitch black, except for a red light dancing against the windows, one of which was broken. Gradually her senses returned. Something terrible had woken her up - terrible, and very close by. She climbed out of bed, fumbled for her dressing gown and slippers, and shuffled towards the bedroom door. From there, she made her way down to the back of the house, and the verandah. Other residents joined her on the way. Wordlessly, they gathered in a small huddle, staring at the flames. Clearly, the little bungalow out the back had scored a direct hit from a stray bomb. It was now a blazing wreck.

*

Bill knelt beside the little stream and placed his sausage-shaped calico bag full of dirt and rock on the ground beside him. He had been poking around this part of the world for months now. The little rivulet was not much more than a trickle, but it was sufficient for his needs. The bag contained nine different samples, each from a different area, and tied off with a string to prevent contamination. He recalled exactly where each one had come from. 'Loaming' was slow and laborious, but it was effective. Untying the first string, he emptied the dirt into his pan, and washed it in the water. There were flashes of gold, no question. He washed the second and third specimens in turn, with similar results. The fourth and fifth looked even better. He must be close now! The last four all also contained gold, but did not look as promising. He scratched his head, looked up the hillside, and planned his next move.

The fires had helped his prospecting enormously. So much of the country that had been unavailable to him earlier, because of the denseness of the vegetation, was now easily accessible. The principal danger - that of limbs falling off gum trees - had largely been removed. They had all burnt. Bill could feel his heart beating with excitement. He needed to stay calm, though. He had not made any great discovery yet, and very possibly never would. Besides, he was now on the Kiewa Fall, where water fell into the Kiewa River. All the old-timers had maintained there was no gold on the Kiewa Fall, and they had certainly spent a lot of time looking. He had only come here himself because he had run out of ideas, and had nowhere else to go. What would become of him if he exhausted all the local possibilities, and found nothing? Would he have to leave the Hotham area, and begin looking elsewhere? Would he simply start again, going over all the same ground?

Bill didn't like to think about that. He had always had faith, and over the last days and weeks that faith had grown stronger. He was up high now, and it wasn't always easy to find enough water for his needs. He had started right down near the river itself. The chance find of a large, moss-covered rock in the river, that looked to be more gold than rock, had given him all the encouragement he needed. True, he hadn't found his prized northern continuation of the Brandy Creek deep lead, but gold on the Kiewa Fall would cause a stir, no doubt about it.

Bill took a few steps up the hill. The sun beat down from a cloudless sky. The steep walls of the gully blocked any wind, and beads of sweat dripped from his bronzed face and arms. A flash on the ground caught his eye. He stopped, moved closer, and looked again. Could it...? Surely not! He walked over to the sparkling rock, and got down on his hands and knees. Gold! Undeniably, it was gold! A rich, gold-studded quartz reef! He had found it! After all the years of struggle and disappointment, he had discovered gold! He rolled over into a sitting position, placed his hands over his eyes, and sobbed. Around him a cluster of red robins, attracted to the newly burnt bush, danced and sang. Bill looked up and gazed at them. How wonderful to have some little friends nearby with whom to share his excitement!

*

On Thursday 12th December 1940, The Herald reported, on page three, under the headline 'Gold Find Reported From Hotham', the discovery of the Red Robin Gold Mine by Mr William Spargo of Middle Plain. Actually, that is not strictly true. The Herald mistakenly referred to it as the 'Red Robert' mine. Bill had already dug almost six feet below the surface, and could see the vein of gold in the rock. He planned to work the mine himself.

*

Less than a month earlier, on 24th November, the German Luftwaffe had commenced night-time firebombing raids on the city of Bristol, approximately 47 miles north of Taunton, where Evelyn was living. The bombing of Bristol was to continue well into the following year, and cause the loss of over a thousand lives. The London Blitz had commenced three months earlier.

33
The Hard Work Begins

Bill glanced at the steep climb ahead, and paused. The thick leather straps cut into his shoulders, and his thighs were screaming. Everything about the mine was so hard! He needed this pot to hold the ore while he crushed, or 'dollied', it with a crowbar. It was extraordinarily heavy, though, and there was no way he could have transported it over to the mine by himself. Placing it in a wheelbarrow was the only solution he could think of. With Eric Johnson pushing, and him out the front pulling, they might just get the job done. That flint hard Norwegian was nearly as crazy as him! This short, sharp pull up to Mt Loch was probably the biggest climb of the journey. If they could manage this, they could get it all the way. He gave a grunt and a wave of the hand, and the two moved slowly forwards once again.

It was a huge relief when the mine finally appeared around the corner. They had made it! The problem now was slowing the barrow down, controlling it on the steep, rocky slope. Every now and then, the barrow bumped into the back of his leg.

Bill came to a stop beside the adit, but gave a cry of anguish as the barrow tipped over sideways. He watched helplessly as, almost in slow motion, the dolly pot rolled over to the lip of the path, and thundered down into the valley below. Bushes and small trees were swept aside or crushed as it smashed its way down the hillside. At last, they could hear it no more. It had come to rest how far down the mountain...400 feet? 500 feet? Bill dropped to his haunches, and placed his hands over his face. How would he ever get it back up again? Johnson kicked a stone from the path, and watched it spin through the air in the wake of the pot.

*

Bill doggedly placed one step in front of another. Occasionally he gave a sharp tug on the rein. The horse didn't seem to be particularly enthusiastic about the task that Bill had given it, and Bill could hardly blame it for that. There were ten large bags, all of them packed with hand-picked, gold-rich ore. They were heavy. Each of the five horses carried two, one on either side of the saddle. Bill had never felt comfortable around horses. They were unpredictable, and they frightened him sometimes.

He would much rather be making this trip with a truck. It was a long, steep climb up to the top of Machinery Spur, and a fair old walk from there, too. The moment he had gained some inkling of the value of his find, he had applied for permission to put a road through from the Alpine Road to the reef. He had received it, too. Road building was something he knew about, but there were no men available to help him. They had all headed down to Melbourne, where they were contributing to the war effort. It was very frustrating. He felt grateful to the Bradshaws for making their horses available to him, and that Jim had agreed to help him bring out the gold-rich bounty he had worked so hard to extract from the ground. It was good to have such friends. There would be other trips on other days. Soon, he would arrange for a large tray truck to come to the Chalet. The ore would then be taken down to the School of Mines in Bairnsdale to be crushed. Exciting times!

A large wedge-tailed eagle soared effortlessly overhead.

*

Bill sat on a simple wooden chair in Polly's Brunswick house. The Herald newspaper rested on his knee, and a cup of tea sat on a small table beside him. He should have been in seventh heaven, but the article made him angry. How dare they! What did they know about him, and who were they to judge, anyway?

So much had happened since the ore had arrived in Bairnsdale. It had given up 173 ounces of gold! Bill was rich! Rich, beyond his wildest dreams! The principal of the school had become very nervous about having so much gold on the premises, however.

The battery was operated by students, and it was impossible to keep a secret like this. He was fearing a robbery at any moment. They had found a bunk for Bill for the night, but he had been urged to sleep with a pistol. Lying there on the mattress with his heart racing, and a gun tucked under his pillow, it was impossible to get much sleep. His mind was racing, too - the past and the future all jumbled up together. Publicity was a two-edged sword. It was wonderful to receive public adulation, but lying alone in the middle of the night worrying about a bullet in the head was not much fun at all. Maybe the smart thing would have been to keep quiet about it all. Ah well, too late to worry about that now!

The train journey to Melbourne had not been much better. It had been generally agreed that the gold bars be placed at the back of the train, in the guard van, and that Bill carry a sugar bag full of sand to serve as a decoy. At least if he was attacked and killed, the thieves would not get the gold. There was some comfort in that, he supposed. Not a lot, though!

Still, he had to admit he felt very proud, as the train was pulling into Spencer Street Station, to hear the platform announcer state that Bill Spargo, the famous gold prospector, was arriving! That was rehabilitation of the family name right there, surely! Nobody could now say that Bill Spargo had amounted to nothing!

He had dressed up specially for the occasion, with coat, tie and hat. He was no dirty bushman. Just because you lived up in the mountains, it didn't mean you couldn't take pride in your appearance. He read the journalist's words again.

I walked into the bank with Mr Spargo who was dressed in shabby old clothes.

The damned cheek of the man! The bank teller had been very condescending, too, assuming Bill had come in to ask for a loan. He had changed his tune quickly enough, when informed of the existence of those massive gold bars! The journalist had described that accurately enough! Ah well, it would not make any difference in the long run. Money spoke in every language, and spoke loudly, too. Bill would have the last word. Besides, he hadn't just deposited gold in the bank during this trip to Melbourne. He had completed a second task, almost as important as the first, and the newspaper had reported that, too. He had sent a telegram - 'reply paid' - to England: STRUCK IT RICH!

"Bill's first camp at the Red Robin"

Horses laden with ore from the Red Robin Mine walking to the Hotham Heights Chalet.

"The Chalet Mt Hotham 6000 ft" (Evelyn's hand)
The Doolan Transport truck loaded with gold-rich ore at the newly built Hotham Heights Chalet (following the 1939 fire), ready to be driven down to the School of Mines in Bairnsdale and crushed.

34
Struck it Rich!

Struck it rich! Evelyn did not know how to feel when she received the news. She was thrilled for Bill, yes, of course. After all these years, he must be absolutely over the moon. She had always thought, if there was any more gold to be found in those mountains, Bill was the one person who could find it. But was there? That was the big question. Well, apparently, there was!

Somehow, though, she did not feel as full of joy as she had expected she would. She was excited, but it all felt so remote and far away. She had supported him for years, yes, and shared his dream, but how could she be ecstatic now, with England being bombed nightly, with the whole of England under threat? The toll on London was appalling, but other cities much closer to home were also being hammered. Would Germany invade England? Even out here in Somerset, was she really safe? Would the Taunton Stop-Line have any effect at all in halting the march of the German Army if it got that far?

And what about Steven? He was nearly 19 years old. It couldn't be long now before he got the call-up from the Navy. She couldn't bear to lose her only child. She had come back to England to be with him, to protect him, but there was nothing she could do to protect him now. Perhaps she should have stayed in Australia. At least she would have been safe there, and his danger would not have been any greater. But life in Australia had lost all its meaning. It had become a tedious, pointless, boring dead end. It was hard to believe she had even ever lived there. That life felt as though it had happened to another person, a long, long time ago.

Bill's excitement reached out to her, but it was so diminished by distance, by the change of circumstances, by the difference between life in England and life in Australia right now, that it barely touched her. It was like a bullet that had been shot high into the sky from the barrel of a rifle, only to land on the ground with a dull thud.

Would she ever see Bill again? Did a life of wealth and comfort truly await her in Australia? Would she even survive the War? Would Steven survive the War? Did she even want to see Bill again?

"Struck it rich!" The telegram had been sent 'reply paid.' What would she say?

35
A New Star in the Heavens

Bill gathered up the wine bottles and placed them in the cupboard. The shelf was nearly full. If it kept up like this, he'd have to find somewhere else to put them. He placed the two juicy T-bone steaks in the Coolgardie safe, along with the various pieces of fresh fruit and vegetables. For days they'd been coming out to his cabin, these men with their fine suits and shiny, patent leather shoes with their slippery soles. They'd arrive looking very weary, and a little the worse for wear. The road was very rough, and had never been properly completed. The last part of the journey had to be made on foot, picking their way through the bush. The one thing in their favour was that the vegetation was still very much reduced because of the fires. They must have been determined, though!

They were enquiring about Bill's favourite foods in Harrietville. Reports were filtering back. Everybody knew he'd been munching on the native herbs and grasses for the last decade. Sorrel. Lots of sorrel. No meat, only fish. Porridge. Potatoes. Onions. Cheese. Anything else was a delicacy, a luxury. Now, suddenly, here it was! Red wine. Port. Steaks. Chops and sausages. Pumpkin. Peas and beans. Tomatoes. Carrots. Proper, healthy lettuces and cabbages, not the pathetic little frostbitten specimens that eked out a marginal existence in his garden. Oh, it was delicious! But even more delicious than the food and wine was the attention. Suddenly, Bill Spargo was somebody! These wealthy men beat a path to his door, they met him on his terms, they answered to his decisions.

Why, he had started a gold rush all on his own! New claims were being pegged on land right around the Red Robin, extending far in all directions. Sure, back in the days when he had managed Hotham Heights, he had also received attention. His efforts to publicise the Chalet saw to that, his photos in the papers, his ads in the skiing magazines. But always he was the servant, succeeding only as long as he remained attentive to the whims and desires of the university students and businessmen. Besides, a career in hospitality was not where his heart lay. The government knew that well enough!

This was different. He was like a little king! Of course, the paperwork always came out towards the end - the pages of contract, the dotted line at the bottom. He had no intention of signing anything, but they didn't know that - and he wasn't about to tell them, either. This was all just too much fun! On one occasion, he had said he wanted to go outside for a walk and a think - and simply not returned! It was well after dark by the time he had come back to the cabin, and it was empty. How long they had waited before finally giving up and deciding to leave was anyone's guess. No doubt he would have heard if they had failed to find their way back. The weather was still mild, after all. They hadn't even had the first snowfall yet. All his life, Bill had been holding onto the wrong end of the stick, with men like these holding onto the other end, the right end. Was it such a bad thing if he chose to relish a few days of revenge? He was like a new star in the heavens, finding its place amongst the others, contributing its own little blaze to the greater glory.

36
Table Tennis

It was his turn to serve. Bill was getting quite good at table tennis, and had just won the last point with a shot that disguised a heavy back spin. The ball had only just made it over the net, only to spin back immediately into it, giving his opponent little chance to return the ball even if he had read the spin, which he hadn't. This recreational sport wasn't such a bad thing at all. He had always dismissed it as frivolous, a waste of time, but now that he had time on his hands, and was no longer anxious about where his next meal was coming from, he could see its appeal. Even back in his teenage days at Mt Wills he had refused to join the local cricket team. Maybe he'd been wrong about that, too... Then again, a man had to eat.

Life was good at the Chalet. There was still too much snow on the ground to go over and resume work at the mine, but that would change soon. The second crushing had been even better than the first. He hadn't bothered to go down to Melbourne this time. The two gold bars had been sent there via registered mail - a bit of a risk, perhaps, but it had worked out all right. No doubt the pattern would continue. It was all very disorienting, this success. Let somebody else worry about the Chalet - stoking the boiler, replacing frozen water pipes, taking out the dunny cans when they were full. It had been good to get away from Mt Hotham for a while during the height of the previous winter. Elsie very generously made her home available for whenever he wanted it, and it was beautiful up in Brisbane during July and August.

The only problem was security. Somebody had stolen a fair amount of gold while he had been away. It hadn't made much of a dent in his profits, but if it continued, it very well might. Everybody was pretty sure who the thief was, but nobody had any proof. Eric bloody Johnson! That bloke was a dead set crook, but what to do about it? He was the only bloke up there anything like as tough as Bill himself, and he was smart enough to cover his tracks. The worst bit about it was that Bill still had to employ him at times! It was the last thing he wanted to do, but there were some tasks Bill just could not manage by himself, and Johnson was the only bloke around who could offer any useful assistance.

Deep in his heart, Bill was worried. Poor Evelyn. He couldn't begin to imagine what she might be going through. She was continuing to write him letters of support, trying to keep the relationship alive, but she was sounding distant, detached, a little uninvolved. Hardly surprising. Even up here, they were not untouched. All signage had been removed so that, if the Japs did make it up here, they would have to work a bit harder to find their way around. A Japanese invasion of Mt Hotham seemed very unlikely, but anything was possible.

Bill was drawn from his reverie. "My serve!" Damn! He had just lost the point!

Bill built a fence around his vegetable garden to keep the cattle out - 1945.

37
The Nurse

Evelyn began unwinding the child's bandage. She was one of the lucky ones. A piece of debris from a bomb blast had struck her in the head, but had not penetrated the skull. The doctor had explained that the wound should eventually heal - children heal very well, after all - as long as the wound did not become infected. The crowded conditions and shortage of supplies made this risk much greater than it would otherwise have been, however. She removed the bandage to expose the layer of gauze that was covering the wound. She had been taught to rinse such wounds with saline on a daily basis, but this was simply not possible. The child began to cry as she started to remove the gauze from the wound. It had dried out, and adhered firmly to the surrounding tissue. The child's mother sat beside her daughter and pinned her arms to her side while Evelyn completed the painful task. She then replaced it with another piece (much thinner than she would have liked), cut the short blood-stained length off the bandage (a new one was out of the question), and re-applied it.

It had made so much sense for Evelyn to answer the advertisements in the papers calling for women to train as nurses. The health service was completely overwhelmed by the War. There was no doubt the need was dire. It also served her own interests in a number of ways. It gave her a strong sense of purpose, a feeling that she was making a worthwhile contribution to the war effort (which she undoubtedly was) and helped her to stop worrying about Steven so much - or at least, manage her anxiety better. It also provided a distraction from her constant ruminations about Bill and, now that events were finally beginning to turn in England's favour, her possible future return to Australia.

38
A Letter from Australia

Evelyn sat in her armchair, the opened letter in her lap. It was another cold, bleak English afternoon. There was so much to think about, now that the War was finally over. After years of doing nothing, simply trying to keep out of trouble and stay alive, the thought of doing anything at all was frightening. She knew, though, she was not the only one feeling like this. People were beginning to move, but their movements were tentative. Besides, food was short, clothing was short, money was short, everything was short - and was likely to stay that way for some time to come.

Lillian was such a wonderful friend, and a very conscientious correspondent. She also knew her main subject - Bill Spargo - well. Bill had proposed marriage to Evelyn by letter. She had not been entirely surprised. It was a logical next step, now that he was wealthy. The head said yes, but the heart was not so sure. It seemed such an enormous move to make. Did she love him? Yes, she did, but it was seven years since she had even seen Bill, and marriage had been the last thing on her mind then. Would she be seen as an opportunist, a gold digger? Surely not, after all the years she had shared his poverty and supported him. And what did she care what people thought anyway? What business was it of theirs? The people that knew her, and cared about her, knew better.

"Marry him, or you will get nothing." The words, in Lillian's beautiful, cursive script, stared out at her from the page - brutal, but honest, and almost certainly correct. Bill was not known for his generous nature. My God, though! There was so much to consider. What about Steven? It had been so sickening to hear that he had been taken prisoner, swimming to shore after his ship had been torpedoed off the coast of Italy. Years of anxiety had followed. Then came the glorious news that he had escaped - and then came the end of the War. A position at Oxford University awaited him, but he had decided to turn it down. That frustrated her. She would have leapt at an opportunity like that at his age. She was still conscious of her lack of education, still opened the dictionary every day and tried to learn a new word.

But Steven was his own man. He had to do what he thought was best for him. He was a free spirit, like herself. The mountains were her muse but, for him, it was the sea. Same disease, different poison. What a ship he had chosen, too! Or was it a boat? The Calista, out of Cornwall. First she had been a tender to Tommy Lipton's J-class yacht Shamrock V, and playing an important role in the 1930 America's Cup challenge. Then she had been involved in the evacuation of Dunkirk in 1940. Now she had been purchased by a Greek millionaire, who was sprucing her up for modern voyages. She was sure to satisfy Steven's lust for adventure.

So, she was heading back to Australia to marry Bill? Is that what she was really doing? Is that what she had decided? There had been nothing left for her in Australia when she had returned to England before the War, but there was nothing left for her in England now, either. And Bill's circumstances were so different! He had done it! He had actually found a rich gold reef, which he had turned into a mine, and was a wealthy man! She still found it hard to believe. It was all so crazy...

She worried about his decision not to sell, though. He was in no position to maximise the mine's potential. Surely, he could see that. He didn't have the capital, and he didn't have the expertise. What did Bill know about mining, really? Prospecting, sure. He had well and truly proved himself in that regard. Passion. Bushcraft. Persistence. These were the keys to success as a prospector, but tunnelling deep into the ground was something else again - very expensive, very labour intensive, and very dangerous. So much had been put on hold during the War. The practical difficulties involved with hard rock mining were probably starting to sink in now.

Bill was such a strange, stubborn man. Would marriage work? Could it work? She couldn't abandon this grand adventure now. Besides, she was tough, too. She had been through a lot, survived a lot, proved herself to herself - and people liked her. She had many good friends. What were her options, after all? She would make it work!

39
Ear Wax

May did not like Bill Spargo. Through the front window, she could see him returning from some unknown and unexplained destination. He was self-centred and pompous. He had no interest in her, and the feeling was mutual. Newly married to Polly's son, Bill Wilson, it made sense for the two of them to live with Polly until they were able to move out by themselves. Bella was with them, too. Her mental health really was not stable enough for her to live by herself.

She could be a bit of a challenge at times, but it was Bill's visits that really rose her hackles. It made her sick to see the way Polly fussed around him, serving up all those beautiful meals which he scoffed like he hadn't eaten for weeks. There was never a word of thanks - not that she ever heard, anyway. He was so secretive, too. He never stayed the night, which was fair enough. There really wasn't room for him, anyway. Where he did spend the night, though, was a complete mystery. Nobody ever talked about it. He was always there next day for another big meal, though.

He was such a snob, too. Wouldn't listen to the "trash" on 3LO. Classical music was the only thing for him, and it had to be up so loud! He looked so silly, sporting that little Charlie Chaplin moustache, and always carrying an umbrella in case it rained. Nobody carried umbrellas. He was such an old woman!

'Hello, Uncle Bill!" she called out as he opened the door.

"You don't need to shout, you know! I'm not deaf!"

May turned away and rolled her eyes. She had seen him nearly hit by a car that he had not heard as he crossed the road that morning. Well, you sure were two hours ago, you old fool, she thought to herself. Why didn't he just say that he'd had his ears syringed?

40
And Do You Take this Man?

He looked so old. That was Evelyn's first impression as she leaned over the rail while the ship nestled into position beside Port Melbourne's Station Pier. Her second impression was the heat, and the harsh Australian sun. No doubt it had made its contribution to the weather-beaten appearance of the small figure who stood below her, just one face in the crowd, but waving so enthusiastically. Yes, of course, much of the time on board ship the weather had been warm, too, but that was just shipboard life. Shipboard life never seemed to be a part of the real world. Now, with the giant hawsers being thrown, and secured around the bollards, reality was settling in once again. It was too late for second thoughts. A flock of seagulls circled wildly overhead, screeching loudly for no apparent reason.

*

There was no time to lose. Bill never felt comfortable in Melbourne, and was keen to return to the mountains as soon as possible. He drove them both straight to St James' Old Cathedral in West Melbourne. The marriage ceremony was efficient and brief. It was 27th February 1946. From there it was on to Scott's Hotel ('the city home of country people'). Bill had booked it on the recommendation of people whose opinion he trusted - not that there were many of those.

*

So much had changed. Gone forever were the bright, breezy days of the 1920s, when everything had been so new and exciting. Even the drab years of the Depression had been better than this. It was the pall of death hanging over everything that made life so sad now. The skiing community had taken a hammering during the War. So had everybody, of course, especially in England, but Evelyn was surprised just how deeply Mt Hotham had changed, too. She was particularly distressed to hear of the death of Fanny Strauss - dear, lovable, kind, gentle, Fanny, killed when the Liberator bomber he was flying crashed into the ocean off northwest Australia.

*

It was a pathetic sight, really. It was worse than doing nothing. If this was the best he could do, he shouldn't have bothered. Evelyn was trying so hard to be positive, to look on the bright side, but it was getting harder and harder. She knew what she was letting herself in for. He didn't have to try to dress it up. She knew she would be picking up where she had left off, no more, no less. These brightly coloured streamers hanging from the ceiling and walls of the cabin did not make the room look festive and cheerful. They looked so out of place, they simply served to heighten the sense of isolation and frugality.

They appeared also to communicate Bill's insecurity, his fear that simply being himself would not be enough, that society's norms needed to be conformed to in a situation like this, that newly married couples were expected to act in a certain way, and that Bill would ensure he had played his part. Hadn't they both breached enough of society's norms already to put Bill at ease on that front? Hadn't they lived together, unmarried, on the very edge of poverty and starvation, in an extremely isolated one room dwelling above the snow line? Hadn't they repeatedly tested the ability of journalists to describe their relationship without provoking a scandal? And hadn't they done all of this without Evelyn falling pregnant? Their relationship must have been a mystery to people for a long time. But had Bill and Evelyn cared about any of this? Hadn't they been confident enough in themselves and each other to simply brush off any such concerns? So why all the pretence now? Why all the false good cheer and forced festivity? Had Bill, like her, simply lost some confidence in their relationship after the years of separation?

Had the traumas and frustrations of the war years damaged his faith in life itself? Perhaps that was it. All was not lost, Evelyn told herself. It was a shaky start, no question, but Bill was still Bill, and Evelyn was still Evelyn. She had loved him before, and she could love him again. She would love him again.

"Mr and Mrs Spargo" - 1946
The newly married couple pose outside the Chalet as the first post-war delivery of ore arrives to be taken down to Bairnsdale.

"Mr Spargo" - 1946
Bill was never comfortable around horses but, once again, he had no choice!

41
Another Log for the Fire

Bill poked his head out from under the blankets, and looked at the fire. He had begun to shiver again. Evening came early on these July afternoons, and the fire was low. He should go outside for another log from the large sawn pile that rested against the end of the hut. Just five more minutes! He looked across at Evelyn in the bunk beside his. From the steady rise and fall of her shoulders, he could see that she had drifted off to sleep. She would wake soon.

He had been excited preparing for this first winter at the mine as part of a married couple. He had sawn an enormous amount of snow gum firewood in preparation. It had crossed his mind to replace the piece of canvas stretched across the end of the hut with a proper wall before the onset of winter, but he hadn't got around to it and now, with snow falling, it was too late. A cool breeze flowed through most of the time.

It had made sense to spend winter at the mine - or so he had thought. He had begun to drive an adit in to meet the reef. This provided protection against the snow. He had lost so much time during the War, when he could not find any assistants to employ, that he was determined now to catch up as much as possible. Of course, no man would join him under these conditions, no matter how much he paid them, and he couldn't expect Evelyn to swing a hammer. She could hold the drill for him while he swung it but, understandably, she tired quickly. The work was painfully slow, but it was better than nothing.

It also allowed him to guard the reef. He was sick of losing gold to thieves. The winter didn't seem to deter them. If anything, it appeared to embolden them, leading them to think there would be nobody else out at the reef to observe their illegal activities.

He was pretty sure who they were - it wasn't just Eric Johnson - but it was very difficult to prove anything. That was the trouble. He couldn't be there all the time, though. The attraction of a short holiday on a beach in Queensland during a Victorian winter was too great to resist. Nevertheless, for now, the gold was safe. It would be impossible for anything to be taken with him and Evelyn camped beside the reef.

Camped. It would be wrong to suggest their style of living was anything more than that. He had always prided himself on his ability to withstand physical discomfort, to cope with any lifestyle, no matter how spartan. But this was testing him like nothing else before. He had to hand it to Evelyn. That woman had guts! She never complained. She had stood beside him unflinchingly in the past, and now she was doing so again. He realised, though, that he had underestimated the difficulty involved. They barely had enough to eat, and were shivering much of the time. He could feel the weight dripping off him, and he had been lean to start with. Ah well! That wood was not going to throw itself on the fire, and it had already been well over five minutes. Bill heaved a big sigh, and threw back the blankets.

42
From a Hospital Bed

Evelyn rolled over and pulled the blankets up under her chin. She had woken once briefly to hear the dawn chorus several hours ago, but had fallen back to sleep, and the sun was now well and truly up. It was time to face the day. She would, too. Soon. It was so wonderful to simply lie in bed and do nothing. She was never cold or hungry in the hospital - just tired. But that, too, would pass eventually.

The weather had eventually defeated them up at the mine. The tail of the winter had been long, and they had begun to run out of food. In the end, Bill had become very anxious for her health. It had only taken a brief break in the weather for him to have decided to try to get them both off the mountain. The walk across to the Chalet, which normally took about two hours, had taken them nearly three, and they were truly exhausted by the time they had arrived. To be truthful, Bill hadn't looked in much better shape than her.

The jeep had really struggled through the drifts of snow on the drive down to Harrietville, and the sleet and wind had whipped their faces mercilessly. Bill had driven her straight to hospital in Fitzroy - nothing but the best now, of course, for a man of his means.

"You'll be right in a week!" he had announced with a great show of bravado as he had left. But a week had passed, and she wasn't right.

She was too tired for visitors, but Aunt Lil was always welcome. Lillian was so well acquainted with all the moving - and stationary - parts of her tumultuous and somewhat chaotic life - Mt Hotham, the Red Robin Mine, and Bill himself. Evelyn had felt she was failing Bill by lying in hospital, but Lillian had assured her that was not the case. Her health came first. She had to look after herself before she could do anything at all to help Bill. Besides, hadn't she already done so much?

The doctor had visited that morning, and expressed considerable anxiety about her general condition. He was particularly concerned that she was underweight. He also believed she was utterly exhausted, both physically and mentally. Her ear would come good, but the drum was still inflamed. She needed time - and no visitors. She was counting on Bill to help her on that score. She had received a letter from him that morning, and wanted to reply as soon as possible. Reluctantly, she pushed the bed clothes down, plumped up her pillows, pulled herself into a seated position, and reached for a pen and paper.

"Hotham Heights looking south at miner's hut"
Could this be where Bill and Evelyn spent the winters of 1946 and 1947?

43
The Scene in Polly's Vestibule

Sunlight streamed through the windows. A peaceful dove cooed softly from a tree outside. The room next to Polly's front door was not large, but it attracted more sunlight than anywhere else in the house, and the four women sat comfortably within it - Evelyn, Bella, Polly's daughter, Elsie, and Polly herself. They all knew what was coming.

Evelyn was in tears. "I couldn't do it."

Memories of her last day at the mine came flooding back. Amazingly, they had returned for a second winter. It had been every bit as gruelling as the first, though they were a little better prepared this time. She was becoming increasingly frustrated, though. Resentful, even. Lillian and Charles lived in that beautiful house at the head of the Ovens Valley. Why couldn't she and Bill move off the mountain, and live in some comfort down below? It was crazy continuing to battle like this. He had the money. It didn't have to be Melbourne. She wouldn't expect that. She wasn't even sure she wanted that. But somewhere near some sort of civilisation. Anywhere but the Red Robin Mine.

The little back door to the hut was low. She had failed to crouch down far enough walking outside to hang the washing that morning, and had struck her head on the frame. Hard. It was the last straw. She had collapsed to the ground in floods of tears, and continued to sob for most of the day. This was it. She had had enough.

Evelyn scanned the faces in front of her. They were all so kind. There was no anger, no bitterness, no resentment. She had feared recriminations, but none appeared to be forthcoming. She had worked so hard to support her husband. She had given her all. Surely they understood! She had withstood so much more than she ever could have imagined she would be able to. Yet still it had not been enough. Nowhere near enough, according to Bill. For God's sake, what did he expect? This was his mine, not hers; his life, not hers.

Evelyn fumbled for her handkerchief to wipe away the tears. Polly offered hers, and she took it.

"I'm so sorry," she repeated. "I just couldn't do it!"

44
A Messy Return

Bill was thrilled when Evelyn and Steven turned up at the mine at lunch time on Saturday, 26th February 1949. Their timing was impeccable. Evelyn knew the rhythms of the mine work intimately, that the men would be knocking off for the weekend just as they arrived. It was wonderful to see them both again, but boy, it was a shock! Hell, Steven had been a little boy when he had last laid eyes on him! Evelyn's departure eighteen months earlier had been messy and distressing for them both. Bill could understand the reason why she had left, though there remained a sense of frustration that she hadn't been able to stick it out.

He wasn't exactly sure why she had returned, but it made sense in a strange sort of a way. The marriage was over. That much was clear. But the friendship was not. They had lived together for too long, they knew each other too well, for that to be the case. If the relationship did have to eventually come to an end, at least there would now be an opportunity to do so in a balanced, civilised, kind way. They owed it to each other, and they owed it to themselves. It was a second chance.

Bill was excited to finally face the prospect of having his own battery, of crushing his own ore. Lillian and Charles had agreed to crush Bill's ore down at their Sambas Mine near Harrietville, but it was exhausting and time-consuming to have to keep carting bags of rock out of the mine. It was undignified, too. The prospect of being fully self-contained was tantalisingly close. Sure, it would only be a small battery and, being so high up the mountainside, water to operate it would always be scarce, but he was sure it would work well enough in time. It was all so hard though - three steps forward and two steps back. He finally had men to work for him, but that had been very difficult. They were all hard-headed, independent men - much like himself. They couldn't be pushed around. It had been damned hard settling on the right wages, too. They all wanted more than he was prepared to pay and, with no clear guidelines to follow, it had been a game of bluff and counter bluff in the beginning. Fortunately, it was all starting to shake itself out now.

Then there had been the massive business of travelling to Melbourne to purchase the battery, and the engine to drive it. He had seen the engine going through its paces at the Show the previous year, and was satisfied with its performance. Eleven days earlier, however, he had received the devastating news that the engine could not be delivered until May. That was hopeless! There would be no time to set it up before the winter, and without the engine, there could be no crushings. He would have to wait until the spring! It was so frustrating. Could he ever really bring all this together? The arrival of Evelyn and Steven was an absolute godsend. On Monday, they would return to Melbourne to buy another engine. All was not lost!

*

Steven was stunned. He could not believe what had happened. He had happily agreed to accompany his mother back to Mt Hotham. He couldn't quite understand why she wanted to go there at all given her appalling experiences as the wife of Bill Spargo, but it was clearly important to her, and he could see that she would benefit from some support. He could perhaps serve a role as a buffer between her and Bill. Besides, he was curious to see the mountain again. He only had dim memories of it from his childhood. He remembered very little of Bill, but from all he had heard he was a stubborn, self-centred man. There was obviously a lot more to him than that, though. After all, he had held his mother in a spell for twenty years. It was only her physical limitations that had brought their relationship to an end. She would do anything for the man - or at least, try to. But he had not expected this! Within minutes of their arrival, they had been drawn deeply into the dilemmas and dramas of his life. They were to spend only two nights on the mountain before heading straight back to Melbourne on an extremely challenging errand! What did he and his mother know about mining engines? This was madness, surely!

*

Bill squatted on the ground, checking through the various components of the battery. He was also keen to erect housing around it as soon as possible to protect it from the elements. The work of bringing all this heavy equipment to the mine was proving to be brutal, though. The men were not happy, and one of the horses had broken down. Evelyn had sent a letter from Melbourne, detailing their progress with the engine purchase. That was one bit of good news. There were problems with the battery, though. Amongst other things, the cam shaft was too short. The anxiety was starting to feel overwhelming. Some problems Bill was able to get around, but you can't add six feet to a cam shaft!

*

Steven arrived back at the mine with his mother. It was Saturday, 19th March - about 5 pm. They had been away almost three weeks. It was good to be on the mountain once again. It had been a difficult challenge to work out exactly what it was that Bill had wanted, but he felt they had acquitted themselves well, and was proud of having done so. It had also proved something of a bonding experience between mother and son. For so much of his life, she had not been with him, and he still didn't feel he knew her all that well. Now, however, he was looking forward to having a good poke around the mine.

*

Bill waited until after dinner to break the bad news.

"The battery arrived while you were away."

He paused.

"The cam shaft is too short. There are other problems, too. I'm sorry, Steven, but you're going to have to return to Melbourne on Monday to sort all this out for me."

Steven looked at his mother. What's wrong with this bloke? How does he cope when we are not around? Clearly, he had no option. It was back to Melbourne for him.

This time, though, he would travel alone. His mother would retire to Bill's old cabin at Golden Point. For her, it was a home away from home.

*

Steven watched as Bill loaded his pack with various pieces of steel equipment to take back to Melbourne.

"Is that all, Bill? Can't you fit the kitchen sink in there somewhere? That pack does not look anywhere near heavy enough for the likes of me. I'm an escaped prisoner of war, you know. This is nothing."

Bill stood up and squinted at Steven through a half-shut eye. He was not amused.

Evelyn giggled. "Don't come back too soon, Steven. Bill is sure to find more problems. Just sit tight and await further orders."

"Very funny. Very funny." Not. Bill was starting to feel irritated. Didn't they understand how critical it was to get the battery fully installed before the onset of winter?

Steven sensed that he had pushed things about as far as they could go - for now. He shouldered the fifty-pound pack on to his back, gave his mother a quick hug, and turned to commence the long plod back to the Chalet.

"Bill Spargo" - 1950
This photo was taken at the Red Robin.

"Red Robin Battery"
The battery always struggled with a lack of water during the summer months.

"Red Robin - Snow squashed water tank at hut"
The hut is the men's quarters at the Red Robin. This is the same hut where Evelyn hit her head emerging through the low door, and collapsed in tears.

45
Life in the Grey Zone

Evelyn enjoyed her twice weekly walks from the Chalet to the mine and back. The two-hour journey gave her plenty of time to think. Sometimes she went three times. Not that she spent all the time deep in thought, of course. The mountains cast their spell over her just as powerfully now as ever, and often she was happy to slip into a hypnotic trance, simply placing one foot in front of another. Other times she admired the view of Mt Feathertop and the Razorback, or watched the fantastic shapes and contortions of the clouds above Mt Loch.

Occasionally she stopped briefly and fixed her gaze on a wedge-tailed eagle riding the thermals. It always reminded her of a story Bill had told her from his days at Hotham before her arrival. He had been distracted by a great bellowing of cows, and had looked up to see four eagles working together to isolate a calf. Two eagles were harassing the calf while the other two kept the herd away from it. Eventually the calf was panicked into running off the edge of a cliff, and falling to its death. She had always found that story hard to believe, but perhaps it was true.

To her right, the pattern of vegetation had made a lasting impression upon her. It was so striking, with the northern slopes of the ridges densely populated with snow gums, while the southern slopes were completely bare. The overall impression was of stripes. No less memorable was Bill's explanation for it, also offered many years ago. The prevailing northerly winds blew the snow onto the southern sides of the ridges, where it lay deeply, and took a long time to melt. There were simply not enough snow-free months on the southern slopes for the seeds to germinate.

Her relationship with Bill had reached a strange stage. Yes, they were married, but they were husband and wife in law only. Indeed, the marriage had begun to die on the very day that it had begun. Yet they were still friends. They still cared about each other. If it was confusing to her, she was sure Bill understood it even less. There was no point in turning to him for guidance.

Yes, she still cared about Bill, and she cared about the future of the Red Robin Mine. She just didn't want to live there, that was all, especially in the winter. That was not so unreasonable, surely? The Chalet was familiar and comfortable. It had been a shock - but ultimately a pleasant one - to first set eyes on the new Chalet that had risen from the ashes of the old...or rather, beside the old one. The stone remnants of the first Chalet had survived in the form of a storage shed, which was rather sad and undignified.

She enjoyed helping at the mine. The men seemed to appreciate her cooking. The cook, Ted Staff, had no previous experience at all, and he didn't set the bar very high. Beef steak and potatoes appeared to be the staple diet. Occasionally some pumpkin. Stewed dried apricots for dessert. Lots of fresh bread, plenty of hot tea, and there was always damper as a last resort. It wasn't hard to improve a little on that. Besides, Ted was happy to get a bit of a break now and then.

There were other small comforts she could provide, too. Ted had told her the trouble he had keeping the flies off the food once it had been prepared. He had asked Bill for some netting to place over the food, but Bill had refused. He could be mean like that. There was no good reason to knock back such a simple request. It had been her pleasure to order some netting from Bright, and have it sent out to the mine. The expression of gratitude on Ted's face had made it more than worthwhile. Bill probably hadn't even noticed.

Yes, she was happy to help Bill at the mine, as long as it was on her terms, and she was able to stay in control - and living at the Chalet allowed her to do that. She had even enjoyed helping him to drive in the wedges in the tunnel to keep the timbers tight, and make sure it was safe for the men. It was simple enough work but critically important, obviously.

Dark clouds were gathering, though. She could feel them. She couldn't live at the Chalet forever. Bill couldn't keep working at the mine forever, either. He was now in his sixties, and a life of brutally hard work and constant exposure to the elements was beginning to take its toll. He would never admit it - possibly not even to himself - but she suspected the failure of their marriage had sapped his spirit, too. Women always coped with such things so much better than men.

What was more, the mine was nowhere near as productive as it had been. They were having to work harder and harder each year for smaller and smaller returns. The remoteness was a challenge. The lack of water in the summer was a challenge. The snow was a massive challenge. Still, there was no point stewing incessantly over the future. It would sort itself out one way or another, she had no doubt about that. There was no harm in simply taking it one day at a time, and enjoying what the life had to offer.

It was Steven who worried her most. He didn't like Bill at all, and made no attempt to hide it. She understood fully the reasons for his animosity, but she sometimes wished he would make some effort to be a little diplomatic. He was almost challenging Bill to confront him. It was potentially an explosive situation.

*

Steven leant back in the little chair, and rested his feet up on the table. The sun was blinding outside, and the hut offered a little relief. He had been reading for a good hour, and was beginning to feel sleepy. He had shoved as much stone as he possibly could into the battery, however, and was confident it would be a long time before he would need to go out and fill it again.

God, this mine was a bore! He had first come here partly out of curiosity, partly out of a sense of loyalty to his mother, but it had turned on him, and become a trap. He hated it now. None of the men had any interest in his world - the great, blue infinite ocean, and the little fishing trawlers that gamely sought each day to extract their rich harvest from its murky depths. Neither did they appear to have any interest in his other great love, the world of literature. It was mining or nothing. If you weren't passionate about mining, you were useless, and an idiot. Simple as that. Struth, even his time looking after the hippos at the Melbourne Zoo had been better than this!

He had made a few attempts to introduce the ocean to the mountains - a hammock for the hut fashioned from knotted rope, a framed picture of a sailing ship to stand on the mantelpiece over at the cabin at Golden Point - but ultimately it was a waste of time. Nobody was interested. There had never been any question of paying him for his labour, either. As the son of his wife, Bill treated him like a member of the family. But he wasn't. He was still getting to know his mother after all those years in the care of her parents. Bill was certainly not a father figure! It didn't matter now how badly he performed as a miner. You can't sack somebody you don't employ!

No, if Steven was going to receive any payment at all for his efforts, he would have to arrange it for himself. Those crates of champagne he had ordered to be delivered to the Chalet when Bill was away for a few days were a good start! He had enjoyed Bill's fury at the discovery that he was going to have to foot the bill more than he had enjoyed the wine itself! And if a little bit of Bill's precious gold made its way into Steven's pocket from time to time, well, who could blame him for that?

*

The sudden crash as the door of the hut slammed open woke Steven abruptly from his slumber. A voice was yelling at him. It sounded like Bill, but it was hard to make sense of anything against the great blinding blur of light.

"What do you think you are doing, overloading the battery like that! The bloody thing seized up, and you haven't even noticed! If it wasn't for your mother, I'd..."

You'd what? thought Steven to himself as he eased himself to a standing position.

*

Bill noted that the little red robins were no longer so evident around the mine. No doubt they had been deterred by the luxuriant post-fire regrowth.

46
Finally, a Plan

Evelyn walked along deep in thought. This time, she was not walking to the mine. Indeed, the thinking was more important than the walking. Evelyn needed to think, and she thought better when she walked. It didn't matter where now, but down the road away from the mine, towards Omeo, was as good as anywhere. It was nice and flat, and she was less likely to be interrupted on this, the quiet side of the mountain.

The mine needed to be sold. As Bill's wife, she was entitled to fifty percent of the proceeds. They both agreed on that. By rights, the mine should have been sold many years ago. Everybody but Bill could see that. The longer he worked it himself, the more its value fell. She had been telling him that for years, but he had refused to listen. Bill had agreed in principle to sell, but had made no attempt to do anything concrete, and they had reached a stalemate. Bill would do nothing more. If Evelyn wanted to extract something from the wreckage, she would have to take the initiative herself.

But what to do? What should be her next step? All she could think of was Lillian. It was Lillian who had advised her to marry Bill, and it was to Lillian she must turn now. Lillian was the uncrowned queen of Harrietville. With her generosity and sense of community, she had long been its spiritual heart. Then, with the death of Charles, only two years after they had married, she had also become wealthy. Proctor's Sambas Mine had just been striking it rich, with a new shoot being discovered, when he had died. The wealth that flowed from this, together with all his other mining interests, and the lovely house they had both lived in at the head of the valley, were now all hers. She was a powerful, highly respected woman.

Not only that, but Bill respected her, too. How could he not? If Lillian came up with concrete plans for the sale of the Red Robin, Evelyn was sure Bill would accede.

47
A Buyer is Found

Lillian sat at the dining room table with her husband, Norm Staff. Norm lacked the gentle charisma and powerful drive of Charles, but was honest, worked hard, and made a satisfactory husband. The older brother of Ted, Norm had worked as a contractor at the mine for the last couple of years, and knew its vagaries well.

Together with John Kenny, Lillian had spent many hours walking up and down Collins Street, trying to find a buyer for Bill's mine. There were no takers. Too much work for too little reward - that was the cry she heard all the time. Kenny, the senior government geologist, had long had a strong professional interest in the Red Robin. However, he had also developed a close personal attachment to both Bill and Evelyn. He had been able to see the point of view of each when the marriage had failed, and had not taken sides. Indeed, in recent times Evelyn had often visited the Kenny household for an evening meal.

Norm could sense what was coming.

"Norm, I can't find a buyer for the Red Robin. I feel a sense of responsibility to Evelyn. After all, it was I who encouraged her to marry Bill in the first place. Would it be such a terrible thing if you and I bought it?"

Norm gave a brief nod.

"No, Lil. That's fair enough."

*

Bill took the news graciously when Evelyn broke it to him. The mine had a buyer. She was leaving. Ah well. This was how it was going to be.

Evelyn had arranged a lift down the mountain for her and Steven. Bill escorted them both back to the Chalet. The mood was sombre. Few words were spoken. Standing outside the Chalet, Bill and Steven shook hands. Bill and Evelyn embraced briefly. Evelyn and Steven climbed into the car, and headed off down the mountain. He never saw either of them again.

A Closing Word

Lillian and Norm Staff purchased the Red Robin Mine from Bill and Evelyn Spargo in 1952 for £12,000. They received £6,000 each. Eleven years earlier, in 1941, Bill had been offered £60,000 for the mine, and probably could have got a lot more.

John (J P L) Kenny (left), Norm Staff (centre, with hands on hips) and Bill (far right) at the Red Robin Mine in 1953

Steven Piper took on work on the great North Sea fishing trawlers, out of Hull, on the east coast of England. Evelyn rented a small apartment in the nearby town of Beverley. Though she never lived in comfort, her share of the proceeds from the sale of the mine funded various real estate investments, and meant she probably did not have to work again. Almeida Russell, the daughter of John (J P L) Kenny, visited her on two occasions. She spoke of Evelyn's warm geniality, but also of her bitterly cold, extremely modest living arrangements.

Steven wrote a book, 'The North Ships - The Life of a Trawlerman', about his time as a fisherman on the North Sea. Sadly, he died, of leukaemia, in 1970, at the age of 47, prior to its publication by David & Charles in 1974. Evelyn saw it through to publication after his death. Before he became ill, he had been planning to embark upon a career as a teacher.

Evelyn Piper died in 1976, at the age of 76. She maintained a strong correspondence with Lillian Staff for many years following her return to England.

Bill sold the hut at Golden Point to Harold Maddison from Porepunkah in 1955. Maddison planned to use the cabin as both a family holiday house, and a base for his own gold seeking. As a holiday destination, it proved a failure. However, he had some success with hydraulic sluicing for gold around the hut. (This explains the coils of canvas hosing.) He died in 1972.

Bill purchased land at Point Lookout at Stradbroke Island in Queensland. There he lived a life very similar to the one he had led at Mt Hotham. (He had spent some time in Queensland every winter since the War.) He became known for his long walks around the rocks, and his desire to 'live off the land', experimenting extensively with the local vegetation and sea life. He built two cottages, which he rented out, and lived in a little room he had fashioned from the stand upon which his water tank stood. Bill discovered brown coal at Point Lookout, and persuaded the Queensland government to mine it, with some success.

Bill and Harold maintained a correspondence after Bill moved to Queensland. (Bill's letters have survived, but Harold's have not.) Bill made it clear he did not believe there was any payable gold left in the vicinity of the cabin. Nevertheless, he encouraged Maddison's gold seeking activities, particularly his plans for hydraulic sluicing, which Bill himself had not explored (though initially he worried about the cost involved in setting it up). Bill provided Harold with detailed advice about where and how to best find gold near the cabin. He made it clear he did not expect a financial share in any finds that Harold might make. They also discussed plans to complete the access road to the cabin, but this was never done. Likewise, plans to install other amenities such as a heater and a hot water service for the cabin were also discussed, but these also never eventuated.

Both Norm and Ted Staff visited Bill on separate occasions. They both believed - wrongly, I am sure - that Bill had discovered another rich gold reef at Mt Hotham. Ted believed it was near the cabin at Golden Point. If he did, the secret died with him. Bill died of stomach cancer, after a short illness, on 7th January 1959, at Mount Olivet Hospital, Kangaroo Point, at the age of 70. His old friend Warrand Begg, long-time President of University Ski Club (and its forerunner, Melbourne University Ski Club), was at his side when he died.

The Red Robin Mine passed through the hands of several owners prior to its closure, under government direction, in 2014. Norm and Lillian sold it to Ken and Claire Harris in 1958. They in turn sold it to two brothers, Frank and John Livingstone in 1963. In 1964, the Livingstones moved the battery down to the West Kiewa River, where there was a much more reliable supply of water. They also built accommodation huts for the mine workers there. Ken Harris jnr. purchased the mine from the estate of the Livingstones in 1978. He built a stone house for his family beside the new battery, to replace the fire-prone buildings that the Livingstones had built. This was completed in 1987. Ken operated the mine until its closure. It is now registered with Heritage Victoria, and has been incorporated into the Alpine National Park. The men's quarters at the mine, where Evelyn had struck her head emerging through the low door in the winter of 1947, were burnt down in the bushfires of 2003.

Spargo's Hut - or cabin, as he called it - at Golden Point was successfully nominated for registration with the Historic Buildings

Council (now Heritage Victoria) by me in 1988. In 2011 the Mt Hotham Resort Management Board created a walking track to connect Spargo's Hut with the resort and two other huts - Derrick Hut and the Silver Brumby Hut. Known as 'The Huts Walk', the construction team was led by Andrew Swift. Swift also drew up extensive plans for the refurbishment of the hut. This was completed in April 2021 by the Victorian High Country Huts Association, with the assistance of the Resort Management Board. The driving force behind the project was Neville Spargo, grandson of Bill's brother, Cecil. Neville was assisted by his son, Ben. Andrew Swift also gave assistance and advice.

A review of the historic photos of the hut shows that considerable changes have been made over time. There is a large patch on the western wall of the hut surrounded by extensive rusting. For a long time, this was a mystery to me. However, early photographs show that Bill built his initial chimney in this location. Members of the work party that refurbished the hut found pieces of what looked like an old stove on the ground nearby. Presumably the arrangement was not a success. (Evelyn's journal notes of 24th March 1934, "...the fire as usual a smoking brute when the wind blows strong...", would appear to attest to this.) No doubt the heat had damaged the galvanised coating of the iron. A new chimney, with a stone hearth, was later built in the current position. There was a tiny room, with a door (perhaps a primitive toilet?), at the far end of the hut, where the chimney now stands. The fence that Bill erected to keep the cattle out of his vegetable garden has long since fallen down. Photos from the 1970s show two extra rooms at the front. These have also fallen down.

The wreck of the Southern Cloud was eventually found in the Snowy Mountains in New South Wales, a long way from Mt Howitt, in 1958, twenty-seven years after it had gone missing.

The framed picture of the sailing ship and the postcard of the red robin featured at the beginning of the book have been lost. If anybody knows where they are, or has seen them recently, I would be grateful if they could get in touch.

A Closing Word

A later photo of Lillian Staff

The hut was wrapped in fireproof foil to protect it from the bushfires of 2019/2020.

This study of Spargo's Hut was painted by renowned skier, painter and raconteur, Bill Rowed.

Ben Spargo, great great nephew of Bill (grandson of Len), standing inside the hut shortly after its refurbishment in 2021.

References

Chapter 12

Pages 45 - 46

Documents held by Public Record Office Victoria

Chapter 31

Page 102

Quote from The Herald, Thursday 9th February 1939, page 6

Chapter 33

Page 109

Quote from The Herald, Monday 7th April 1941, page 7

Photo credits

Bill took many photographs, and where a photo appears likely to have been taken by him, I have credited him as the photographer. Most of the photos of Evelyn, I am sure, would have been taken by Bill; likewise most of the early photos of the Chalet in winter. I am unclear how many photographs Evelyn took. It is possible that some of the uncredited photos should have been credited to her. Photographs that do not appear in the following list were taken by me.

"We are found..." (photo by W. B. Spargo, courtesy Kate Piper) - Page 9

Picnic Point Brewery (courtesy State Library Victoria) - Page 12

The Spargo Children: Polly, Bill, Cecil and Elsie (courtesy Dianne Carroll - High Country Heritage/Pioneer Portraits) - Page 12

"Hanging out the clothes 1930" (photo by W. B. Spargo, courtesy Kate Piper) - Page 16

Evelyn standing in front of the weather station... (photo by W. B. Spargo, courtesy Kate Piper) - Page 16

Evelyn with Trixie (photo by W. B. Spargo, courtesy Kate Piper) - Page 16

Evelyn racing down a slope (photo by W. B. Spargo, courtesy Kate Piper) - Page 19

Evelyn taking a tumble (photo by W. B. Spargo, courtesy Kate Piper) - Page 19

"Cecil Spargo 100 Wilson Street, Brunswick" (photographer unknown, courtesy Neville Spargo) - Page 26

Bill Spargo - studio portrait (courtesy Ross and Jean Goldsworthy) - Page 26

"Evelyn Falls, Hotham Heights, Victoria" (photo by W. B. Spargo, courtesy Kate Piper) - Page 26

"My Favourite Picture of Hotham Heights" (photo by W. B. Spargo, courtesy Miriam Barber) - Page 27

"Hotham Heights" Chalet in Summer (courtesy Royal History Society of Victoria) - Page 27

Members of the Melbourne Walking Club... (courtesy Royal Historical Society of Victoria) - Page 28

"A party of ski-ers at Hotham in August 1929" (photo by W. B. Spargo, courtesy Sam Piper) - Page 28

"Snow drifts intersect the Alpine Rd in summer months..." (photo by W. B. Spargo, courtesy Sam Piper) - Page 28

Bill's motorcycle (photo by W. B. Spargo, courtesy Miriam Barber) - Page 29

"The Edge of Beyond" (photo by W. B. Spargo, courtesy Kate Piper) - Page 29

Steven with the dogs (courtesy Kate Piper) - Page 32

Bill and Steven (photo by E. M. Piper, courtesy Kate Piper) - Page 33

"The Young Geologist 1930" (photo by E. M. Piper, courtesy Kate Piper) - Page 33

"On the Rocky Road to Little Plains Summer 1932" (photo by W. B. Spargo, courtesy Kate Piper) - Page 44

"On ramp at Hotham Heights..." (photo by W. B. Spargo, courtesy Ross and Jean Goldsworthy/Kate Piper) - Page 64

"Mt Loch and Mt Feathertop above the clouds Aust Alps" (courtesy Kate Piper) - Page 76

Bill building the first chimney... (photo by E. M. Piper, courtesy Kate Piper) - Page 82

Evelyn wringing out clothes... (photo by W. B. Spargo, courtesy Kate Piper) - Page 82

"Nature forms this old Snow Man..." (courtesy Kate Piper) - Page 83

"See the herring-bone tracks of the skis..." (courtesy Kate Piper) - Page 83

Skis with fish (courtesy Kate Piper) - Page 84

"Crossing the creek with the mails..." (photo by W. B. Spargo, courtesy Kate Piper) - Page 84

Evelyn swimming (photo by W. B. Spargo, courtesy Kate Piper) - Page 84

"Forking the channel" (photo by W. B. Spargo, courtesy Kate Piper) - Page 85

Evelyn holding frying pan (photo by W. B. Spargo, courtesy Kate Piper) - Page 85

Spargo's Hut... (courtesy Kate Piper) - Page 85

Evelyn enjoying the view... (photo by W. B. Spargo, courtesy Kate Piper) - Page 86

The structure beside the chimney... (photo by W. B. Spargo, courtesy Kate Piper) - Page 86

Evelyn peeping out... (photo by W. B. Spargo, courtesy Kate Piper) - Page 86

Evelyn in snowshoes beside the hut... (photo by W. B. Spargo, courtesy Kate Piper) - Page 87

I wonder if the structure... (courtesy Kate Piper) - Page 87

"At Hotham 1937" (photo by E. M. Piper, courtesy Kate Piper) - Page 87

"Starting of the first tunnel, Nov 1933, on the Vic Alps" (photo by W. B. Spargo, courtesy Kate Piper) - Page 92

The burnt out remains... (courtesy Harrietville Historical Society)- Page 99

"Bill's first camp at the Red Robin" (courtesy Rob Kaufman) - Page 110

Horses laden with ore from the Red Robin Mine... (photo by W. B. Spargo, courtesy Kate Piper) - Page 110

"The Chalet Mt Hotham 6000 ft" (photo by W. B. Spargo, courtesy Kate Piper) - Page 111

Photo credits

Bill built a fence around his vegetable garden... (courtesy Mick Hull) - Page 117

"Mr and Mrs Spargo" - 1946 (photo by Marjorie Byron Moore, courtesy Fred Ward) - Page 125

"Mr Spargo" - 1946 (photo by Marjorie Byron Moore, courtesy Fred Ward) - Page 125

"Hotham Heights looking south at miner's hut" (courtesy Geological Survey of Victoria historical photograph collection) - Page 129

"Bill Spargo" - 1950 (courtesy Ted Staff) - Page 136

"Red Robin Battery" (courtesy Ted Staff) - Page 137

"Red Robin - Snow squashed water tank at hut" (courtesy Ted Staff) - Page 137

John (JPL) Kenny (left), Norm Staff (centre, with hands on hips) and Bill (far right) at the Red Robin Mine in 1953 (courtesy Geological Survey of Victoria historical photograph collection) - Page 145

A later photo of Lillian Staff (courtesy Harrietville Historical Society) - Page 149

This study of Spargo's Hut... (courtesy Nan Rowed) - Page 150

Ben Spargo, great great nephew of Bill... (courtesy Neville Spargo) - Page 150

Author photo on back cover by Maggie Somerville

Photo of hut refurbishment work party on back cover courtesy Graham Gales

Portrait of Bill Spargo on back cover courtesy Dianne Carroll - High Country Heritage/Pioneer Portraits

Portrait of Evelyn Piper on back cover by W. B. Spargo (courtesy Kate Piper)

Cover photo of currawong by W. B. Spargo (courtesy Kate Piper)

Newspapers featuring Bill's photographs

First Pictures of Mt. Hotham Snow Sports (The Sun News-Pictorial, Wednesday, May 15 1929, page 1)

Where The Telephone Linesman's Job Is Chilly (The Sun News-Pictorial, Friday, June 14 1929, page 1)

Victoria's Snow-clad Alps - Special Pictures (The Herald, Friday June 14 1929, page 22)

Captions of newspaper photographs

First Pictures of Mt. Hotham Snow Sports

WINTER'S WHITE MANTLE HAS SPREAD ITSELF OVER MOUNT HOTHAM. -- First photographs of this season's snow sports at the Mount where the falls of snow are lasting and safe. Here the Ski Club makes its rendezvous. The road from Omeo is still open to cars, but drift snow blocks the St. Bernard road. The top picture is of a ski and toboggan party on the side of Mount Hotham. The lower photograph shows a happy advance party of snow enthusiasts.

Where The Telephone Linesman's Job Is Chilly

TELEPHONE LINES BECOME ROPES OF ICE on the freezing heights of Hotham, and are easily snapped by a strong wind. To preserve telephone communication in spite of snow and blizzard during the winter is no easy task, but this season the Postmaster-General's Department has taken special precautions to achieve that end. This picture shows a break in the line between the Hospice and the Cottage on the heights.

LIKE SCENES IN SNOWY SWITZERLAND are the prospects on Mount Hotham. Snow now lies two or three foot deep over an area 18 miles wide in the district. Left: A linesman from Omeo repairing the telephone wire just outside Hotham Heights Cottage, where breaks are frequent owing to snow and high wind. He has been fully supplied with skis, light ladder, and all necessary equipment for travel and work in the snow. Right: The Cottage as it is today. These pictures arrived in Melbourne yesterday.

Victoria's Snow-clad Alps -- Special Pictures

THE BIG BLIZZARD ON THE VICTORIAN ALPS: This series of special photographs, taken by a Herald photographic correspondent in the neighbourhood of Hotham Heights, gives an excellent idea of the severe snow blizzard which has been raging on the Victorian Alps during the last few days. The photograph on the left shows the meteorological recording instruments from which the depth of snow and the weather conditions are sent daily to headquarters in Melbourne. On the right is the beautiful effect obtained by a stunted snow-gum borne down by the weight of snow. A fall of three feet six inches has been reported from Mount Hotham.

A WONDERFUL VISTA OF SNOW AND CLOUD: The remarkably fine photographic study on the left shows, in the foreground, the snow-covered top of Mount Hotham, with the rolling vista of mountain ranges going away in the distance towards Feathertop. On the right two telephone linesmen who have been instructed in the use of ski are seen beside the only line which affords communication with the outside world from Mount Hotham and St. Bernard. The G.P.O. men are now engaged in repairing sections of the line which have been damaged by the recent heavy snowfall. The fantastic effect produced by the icicles attached to the telephone pole will be noted.

Acknowledgements

My son, Thomas, has accompanied me on many walks to Spargo's Hut and the surrounding country during his childhood and later years. We have skied the slopes around Mt Hotham together for almost as long, and continue to do so. He has grown to share my love of the high country, the subject of alpine history, and my fascination with the story of Bill and Evelyn in particular. He has also given me very helpful advice in relation to the publication of this book.

My daughter, Lenore, has also walked to Spargo's Hut with me, and accompanied me and Thomas on many other walks in the high country. She has also skied with Thomas and me since her childhood. Both Thomas and Lenore gave me valuable advice about the cover of this book. Lenore also drew a sketch of Spargo's Hut from one of my photographs, and presented it to me on my birthday. It is one of my most treasured possessions.

I wish also to thank Maggie Somerville, who strongly encouraged me to write the book sooner rather than later, before I became too old, and ran the risk of suffering ill-health. She has followed my progress closely since then, and continued to give me every encouragement, as well as valuable feedback on the manuscript.

I wish to thank the late Edel Wignell for her support and encouragement, for proofreading the manuscript, and for providing a number of helpful suggestions.

I wish also to thank Sylvia Whiteside for her support in the early stages of the project.

Thank you also to Sue Robertson for pushing me to write the book sooner rather than later.

I am extremely grateful to Ian Stapleton for his assistance and support over many years. Not only were his books of great value, but he has been a highly reliable and supportive sounding board over both the research and the writing stages of the project.

I wish to thank the late Nancye Sullivan also for her support in the early stages of the project. Nancye provided me with important documents relating to the purchase of the hut by her late father, Harold Maddison, from Bill in 1955. She also gave me letters received by her father from Bill when he was living on Stradbroke Island, important documents relating to the original construction of the hut, and other documents relating to Bill's various mining activities.

Thank you to Pat Keogh, my physiology tutor when I was a medical student, for her stories about the early days of the Victorian skiing industry, for providing me with access to the early skiing publications, and for helping me to get started.

I wish to thank descendants of Evelyn's family - her daughter-in-law, Priscilla Batcheldor, and her grandson (Priscilla's son), the late Sam Piper. They provided me with valuable information - in the form of letters, emails and photographs - over several decades. More recently, Sam's daughter, Kate, has also provided me with invaluable information in the form of photographs, letters to and from Evelyn, and some of Evelyn's journal entries. Bill's grandnephew, Neville Spargo, has also offered me great support in recent times, and made a number of helpful suggestions. Neville, Priscilla and Kate, to my great relief, have all approved the manuscript.

Thank you to Wendy Cross for her encouragement, and for providing important information relating to Evelyn. Thank you to Clive Willman for technical advice relating to mining, and for providing me with access to the historical photograph collection of the Geological Survey of Victoria. Thank you also to Ken Harris, former, and most recent owner of the Red Robin Mine, for his enthusiasm and helpful suggestions. Ken, I am pleased to say, also approved the manuscript. Thank you to mining heritage consultant Andrew Swift for important information about Bill's various activities. Likewise, the late Neville Wolff provided me with much helpful information.

Thank you also to Professor Peter Stanley, who read the manuscript, and made numerous helpful suggestions (and picked up a critical error!).

Thank you to my dear friend, Dr Peter Fullagar, who also reviewed the manuscript and provided valuable feedback.

Thank you to English story consultant and author David Baboulene whose online writing course showed me how to write this book.

I wish to thank the Harrietville Historical Society for providing me with access to their wonderful collection of photographs.

Thank you to the Public Record Office Victoria for providing me with access to documents relating to Helmut Kofler's time at Mt Hotham, and to the termination of Bill's Country Roads Board lease. Thank you to National Archives Australia for salvaging a number of damaged historic photographic negatives received from Kate Piper. Thank you to Action Replay for digitising the microcassettes that contained the recorded interviews, and to Hillvale Photo and Image Science for digitising the photographic negatives.

I wish to especially thank the people who allowed me to interview and record their memories of Bill and/or Evelyn. They welcomed me into their lives, and gave very generously of their time and thoughts. I have listed their names at the back of the book. Ross and Jean Goldsworthy allowed me to dictate Evelyn's "Elegy" onto my Dictaphone recorder.

I wish also to thank the many people who spoke to me on the phone about Bill and Evelyn. They are too many to list here, but they all had useful information to impart and, with very few exceptions, did so generously.

Thank you to Fiona Sinclair for a beautiful cover design.

Finally, I wish to thank Kev Howlett and Les Zigomanis at Busybird Publishing for helping me to put this book together. Thank you especially to Kev for his unfailing courtesy and patience.

List of recorded interviews

05/04/1987: Ted and Bunty Staff

Ted Staff worked as the cook at the Red Robin Mine for three months in the summer of 1949/50

09/04/1987: Mick and Shirley Hull

Mick and Shirley Hull were pioneering skiers. Mick first skied at Mt Hotham in 1934.

26/04/1987: Fred Ward

Fred Ward drove skiers to Mt Hotham from Omeo in the years after World War 2. He was also a gold prospector.

29/04/1987: Almeida Russell

Almeida Russell was the daughter of the Chief Government Geologist, J P L Kenny. She was also a good friend of Evelyn Piper.

05/05/1987: Alma Coleman

Alma Coleman was a pioneering skier, and a foundation member of Edelweiss Ski Club.

07/05/1987: Bill and May Wilson

Bill Wilson was Bill Spargo's nephew. (He was the son of Bill's sister, Polly.) May was his wife.

List of recorded interviews

13/05/1987: Martin Romuld

Martin Romuld was a Norwegian-born engineer who worked on the Kiewa Hydroelectric Scheme in the 1930s. He was also a champion skier.

21/05/1987: Harold Doughty

Harold Doughty was a skiing pioneer.

21/05/1987: Gordon Brown

Gordon Brown was a skiing pioneer.

24/05/1987: Charlie McNamara

Charlie McNamara was a cattleman. He lived at Cobungra, and then Omeo. Charlie knew Bill Spargo well.

11/06/1987: Pearl Bradshaw

Pearl Bradshaw managed the Hotham Heights Chalet with her husband, Jim, from 1937 - 45.

11/06/1987: Len Spargo

Len Spargo was Bill Spargo's nephew. (He was the son of Bill's brother, Cecil.) Len lived at Hotham Heights Chalet from 1929 - 33.

14/06/1987: Gordon Brown (second interview)

21/06/1987: O C Smith

O C Smith was a mining surveyor. He surveyed the Red Robin lease for Bill Spargo in 1941.

02/07/1987: Elsie and Herb Clark

Elsie Clark was Bill Spargo's niece. (She was the daughter of his sister, Polly.) Herb was her husband.

12/07/1987: Les Woodard

Les Woodard worked for Bill Spargo on the Alpine Road in the 1920s.

26/07/1987: Ross and Jean Goldsworthy

Ross and Jean Goldsworthy managed the Hotham Heights Chalet during the winter of 1933.

15/10/1987: Pat Keogh

Pat Keogh was a pioneering skier, active with the University Ski Club from the early post-war years. She was also my Physiology tutor when I was a medical student.

17/10/1987: Bill Callander

Bill Callander was a pioneering skier, and a foundation member of the Wangaratta Ski Club.

09/11/1987: Pearl Bradshaw (second interview)

06/12/1987: Joyce Fraser

Joyce Fraser grew up on Cobungra Station, a historic cattle property. Bill Spargo visited often when she was a child.

14/02/1988: O C Smith (second interview)

List of recorded interviews

14/02/1988: Vic Attridge

Vic Attridge was a cattleman and a miner. He lived at Harrietville.

20/03/1988: Niall Brennan

Niall Brennan was a writer who wrote about the history of the Australian Alps. He met Bill Spargo on one occasion.

12/06/1988: Marion Barber

Marion Barber was Joyce Fraser's older sister. She also lived at Cobungra Station, and knew Bill Spargo.

20/10/1988: Martin Romuld (second interview)

About the Author

Stephen Whiteside has been walking and skiing through the Australian mountains for most of his life. He has also been writing for many years - mostly rhyming verse, but also short stories, and articles about Australia's history and natural environment. Many of his poems have been published in magazines or anthologies, both in Australia and overseas, or won awards. In 2014, Walker Books published a collection of his poetry for children, *"The Billy that Died with its Boots On and other Australian Verse."* In 2015, the book won a Golden Gumleaf for "Book of the Year" at the Australian Bush Laureate Awards during the Tamworth Country Music Festival. Whiteside works as a GP in Melbourne. This is his first novella.

Previous books by Stephen Whiteside

The Billy That Died With Its Boots On and Other Australian Verse (Walker Books, 2014)

The "Ant Explorer" Parodies (self-published, 2010)

"The Brigadier's Horse" and other poems from the Western Front by Arthur Dean, compiled by Stephen Whiteside (self-published 2010)

The Paterson Parodies (self-published 2009)

Poems of 2008 (self-published 2009)

Early Poems and Songs (including "Omeo") (self-published 2008)

Poems of 2007 (self-published 2008)

More information can be found, and copies of "Snow, Fire and Gold" can be purchased, at **snowfireandgold.com.au**

www.ingramcontent.com/pod-product-compliance
Lightning Source LLC
Chambersburg PA
CBHW041307110526
44590CB00028B/4272